The ESSENTIALS of

Buying & Selling
A Business

Verne A. Bunn

**And the Staff of Research and Education Association
Dr. M. Fogiel, Director**

Research & Education Association
61 Ethel Road West
Piscataway, New Jersey 08854

THE ESSENTIALS®
OF BUYING & SELLING A BUSINESS

Printed in the United States of America

Library of Congress Catalog Card Number 99-70106

International Standard Book Number 0-87891-245-2

Foreword

THE PERSON who plans to go into business for himself faces a great adventure—or a great disaster. Which it will be depends a great deal on how well he prepares himself through investigation and analysis of the situation he is about to enter.

In some ways, the person who buys a going business has an advantage over the one who starts from scratch. For one thing, he has more facts to work with—*if* he knows where to find them and how to use them.

These are the principal problems taken up in *Buying and Selling a Small Business*. What should the prospective buyer of a small business—or the seller—know before the buy-sell decision is made? Where can he find this information? How can he correlate and interpret the data he collects? How does he apply what he learns to negotiating a buy-sell transaction?

This volume does not pretend to give complete or specific answers—in some cases professional help is necessary, and in all cases the answers depend on many variables. It is intended rather to serve as a guide to areas needing investigation and to suggest some approaches that may be helpful.

The buyer of a small business faces more problems—and more difficult ones—than the seller. Because of this, *Buying and Selling a Small Business* may appear to give more attention to the buyer than to the seller. However, it is important for the seller to know how the buyer is likely to approach the negotiations; and wherever specific problems for the seller do come into the picture, they are discussed separately.

Contents

Part 1

The Buy-Sell Transaction

Chapter 1

A Small Business
Is Bought and Sold

Is THERE A SMALL-BUSINESS OWNER who has never considered selling his business? Probably not. Is there an individual with some money, talent, or an urge for independence (often only the last) who hasn't thought about owning his own business?

The number of small businesses actually bought and sold, however, represents only a small fraction of those who have felt these urges. To many people, the desire to buy or sell is only a passing thought. Others find various ways to solve their problems or satisfy their ambitions. But sometimes an individual doesn't follow through because he finds the prospect of buying or selling a business too baffling.

The objective of this book is to describe the process of buying and selling a small business and to establish some guidelines. It will not remove the difficulties, but it will make them more manageable.

A Look at the Buy-Sell Process

It will be helpful to take a detailed look at what happens when a business is bought or sold. First, consider some of the thoughts that go through the minds of the buyer and seller during the decisionmaking process.

THE SELLER: (*Before the transaction*) Shall I sell my business? What is it worth? How can I find a buyer? (*During the transaction*) How much shall I tell this guy about my business? Will he raise his offer? What terms shall I insist on? (*After the transaction*) Should I really have sold? I wonder if I could have got more money. Wonder how the business is getting along.

THE BUYER: (*During the transaction*) Shall I buy this business? I wonder why he *really* wants to sell. How much can I afford to pay? Where can I get the rest? How far will he reduce his price? (*After the transaction*) Now that I've bought it, which new idea shall I try first? Should I have known *that* would happen? It's going to work out just fine—*isn't it?*

These are typical thought patterns. They mark the flow of decisions in the transaction. They also reflect the doubts and hesitancy involved in the decisionmaking.

A Step-by-Step Account

The following step-by-step description of buying and selling a grocery store is basically the story of an actual case. To make it more typical of all buy-sell transactions, some questions and problems from other cases have been worked into the account.

Bill Smith [1] wants to buy. Bill Smith had worked several years in grocery stores in Whitton, a city of 300,000. He had started as a carry-out boy and progressed through every job in a store operation.

Bill was anxious to own his own store. He and his wife were in their early forties and eager to establish a business of their own. They had saved about $8,000, and Bill was confident that he knew enough about grocery stores to handle the operation. His wife planned to take care of the bookkeeping.

The Smiths had followed up many leads from the classified section of the newspaper. In every case, they found the business either too run down to salvage or too large to finance. Bill had also talked to a few real estate agents who specialized in business properties. But the agents' listings had not turned up anything that interested the Smiths.

In August, Bill learned from a food salesman that Sam Brown was trying to sell his store. Sam's Market was a small store on the other side of town. It had been operating for many years.

Sam Brown wants to sell. Sam Brown had been thinking about selling his business for several months. He was reluctant to do it because the store had been established by his father. Yet he was finding the long hours he had to spend in the store a real hardship.

Furthermore, during the last 4 years, business had declined from a high of $200,000 gross sales to less than $100,000. The main reason

---

[1] Names in all examples have been changed.

for the decline in sales, in Sam's opinion, was the competition from several new supermarkets in his area.

Finally, he was concerned about a space of about 1,100 square feet at one end of the building in which the store was located. Sam owned the entire building and had been unable to find a tenant for this space for more than 3 months. Now a discount paint company had offered him a local franchise.

Sam believed he could use the vacant space for this operation and handle the business with much less effort than he was putting into the grocery store. If he could sell the grocery business and lease that part of the building to the new owner, he would have a comfortable arrangement.

The transaction. After talking to the salesman, Bill called Sam and expressed an interest in the store. They arranged several meetings to discuss the situation. Bill learned that Sam wanted to sell in order to take advantage of the paint-store opportunity. When Sam announced that he was asking $25,000 cash and $300 a month rent, the conversation went like this:

BILL: Could I spend some time with your books?

SAM: I can't let you do that. Most of my personal affairs are in those books. Besides, I don't want to be giving away everything about my business to someone who might be a competitor someday.

BILL: But I have to have something to go on!

SAM: Well, you ask me what you think you need to know, and I'll tell you—if I can.

During the discussions that followed, Bill learned the following facts about the store:

The modern fixtures and equipment had cost $30,000 new. Now 6 years old, they had a depreciated value of $15,000. The inventory had a wholesale cost of $10,000. Gross sales were running about $8,000 a month with a gross margin between 14 and 16 percent. In the past, annual sales had been as high as $200,000. The 3,900 square feet of store space appeared well organized.

From this information and his observation of the store, Bill figured that he could increase sales to $20,000 a month within a year by more aggressive sales promotion—handbills, radio spot announcements, an extra large neon sign, and more personal service. This meant, in Bill's opinion, that inventory would need to be enlarged to $12,000.

To better the profit, which had been averaging 2½ percent of gross sales including Sam's salary, Bill believed the average markup should be raised from 18 percent to 20 percent. An additional increase in profit could be realized, according to Bill's analysis, if he reduced the staff by one full-time and one part-time clerk.

Bill was unable to borrow the difference between his $8,000 savings and Sam's asking price of $25,000. Several banks turned him down before one agreed to lend him $10,000 at 8 percent interest with monthly payments over 5 years.

Sam refused Bill's offer of $18,000 but offered to carry part of the price. After several more discussions, agreement was reached on the following terms:

1. $12,000 cash.
2. $11,000 unsecured note, payable monthly over 5 years at 8 percent interest.
3. $200 a month rent.

Bill planned to use the $6,000 cash left from the bank loan to increase inventory and provide working capital.

The store changed owners about September 1. Bill discovered that the inventory was worth only $8,000 at wholesale cost. He immediately used $4,000 to increase his shelf stock. Sales during the first few months increased to $15,000 a month, and Bill felt sure he could reach his goal of $20,000 a month. Profit, however, was running only 2 percent of gross sales in spite of Bill's attempt to increase margins and reduce costs.

A sad ending. Six months later, the doors were closed on Bill's Market. The remaining $6,000 inventory was sold to a wholesale outlet for $5,400. The fixtures were sold for $8,200. Bill was trying to find a way to pay his debts and forget the loss of his life's savings.

Four months later, Sam still had not been able to rent the space formerly occupied by the food store. He had little prospect of recovering his loan to Bill, and he had lost over $2,000 in rental income. He was undecided what action he should take.

The Big Question

Bill and Sam each thought he had received a fair value. But the final result showed that neither one had made a right decision. Both lost savings and income. What went wrong? How do you go about buying or selling a business?

An important question? To the Bills and Sams—past, present, and future—few questions could be more important.

A difficult question? Either buying or selling a business requires personal, financial, and management decisions. At no steps along the way are the decisions easy to make. But it will be helpful to establish the basic steps or elements in a buy-sell transaction and then to examine each of these elements.

Chapter 2

The Flow of Decisions
in a Buy-Sell Transaction

Buyers and sellers both seek answers to the same question: "What is this business worth?" Most people see the worth of a business as the total value of equipment and fixtures, inventory, and buildings and land. Important, certainly, but the sum of these values does not equal the value of the business.

Bill probably paid a fair price for equipment, fixtures, and the like. But did his price of $23,000 reflect the value of Sam's Market? Obviously not. What, then, *is* the value of a business?

For both buyer and seller finding the answer to this question is the most difficult and at the same time the most important step in the buy-sell process. But this final decision reflects many other decisions made while the transaction is being considered. In other words, the buy-sell process is a flow of decisions. It would be impossible to point out every decision that must be made, but the basic ones are as follows:

Motivation: a decision to attempt the sale or purchase of a business.

Contact: a decision on how to find a buyer (or seller) for a business with specified characteristics.

Information: a decision on what information must be gathered or given to buy or sell a business.

Sources: a decision on how, where, and at what cost the needed information can be obtained.

Analysis: a decision on the meaning, importance, and reliability of the information gathered.

Value: a decision on what the business is worth.

Price: a decision on how much money to take or give for the business.

Financing: a decision on how to pay or receive the purchase price.

Contract: a decision on the form and content of the contractual relation.

Implementation: a decision on how and when to effect transfer of ownership.

Motivation

What leads an owner to *sell* his business? It may be any of a large number of reasons: a personal health problem, a business disagreement, overextension of the company's activities, a desire to retire from business. The possible reasons are many and varied.

For Sam, the motivating factor was change. He found his sales decreasing in spite of his extra effort, competition increasing, empty building space impossible to rent. In other words, both internal and external factors had brought changed conditions that affected the business unfavorably.

Changed conditions should be analyzed carefully before a business owner accepts them as reasons for selling his business. The following questions can serve as a guideline for this analysis:

1. Have changes actually occurred in my business?
2. Are the causes of the changes beyond my control?
3. Are the causes of the changes within my control?

It would be unfortunate for a owner to sell his business because of changes he could control if, by such control, he could recapture a successful and satisfying operation. Every owner, therefore, should examine closely his motives for wanting to sell the business.

What makes an individual want to *buy* a business? Again, motivations will cover the whole range of human desires, from simple economic gain to social ladder climbing.

Bill's prime motivating factor was the desire to expand a special skill into a business of his own. Bill thought he knew enough about grocery stores to handle one of his own. But he didn't. This factor of a special skill represents one of the dominant reasons for wanting to buy a business. It is a natural motive but, perhaps because of its natural appeal, it can be a dangerous motive.

A business must be *managed*. An operating skill does not always lead to managing ability. In fact, it often encourages a business owner to spend his time operating instead of managing. Planning for the future, organizing resources, staffing the business with competent people, directing the coordination of people and operations, controlling results—these are the functions of management. Consequently, an individual with a skill seeking to buy a business in which to apply the skill should check his motivation by asking questions such as the following:

How important is management ability in this business?

Occasionally, a business that is unique and very simple almost manages itself. But if the business is in a competitive field, management ability is probably the most important requirement for success.

Do I have the ability to manage successfully?

Effectiveness with people (customers and employees), eagerness to tackle difficult problems and make decisions, and intelligence about general business operations are key ingredients in management ability.

Can I learn how to manage this business?

Most people can learn to manage if they recognize the need. This requires room to make mistakes, however, and the self-discipline to undertake self-improvement programs.

Contact

Assuming that motives have been examined and that both seller and buyer are still interested, the next step is to get the two together. But there seems to be no "best way" to find a seller or a buyer for a business.

From the seller's point of view, the task of finding an interested buyer is the more difficult one, but there are many avenues to explore other than running advertisements in newspapers. He should ask himself these questions:

> Have I told my employees and other business associates that I intend to sell the business?
>
> Have I taken advantage of the broadcasting ability of salesmen who call on businesses similar to mine, of association meetings, of other trade contacts?

This informal advertising requires the same kind of information more formal advertising does. Business associates, trade contacts, and friends should be told the asking price, the terms, the anticipated return. Without this knowledge, a potential buyer can hardly be expected to respond positively. He needs to know in advance how the offer relates to his financial ability.

From the buyer's point of view, finding opportunities is relatively easy. The difficulty lies in locating a business he can analyze confidently. When he deals with unfamiliar firms, he is haunted by a desire for more information and suspicious about the information he does receive. A buyer seeking a seller should consider the following points:

> Have I asked people I deal with about persons who might be considering selling a business?
>
> Have I considered approaching businesses with which I am familiar about the possibility of a purchase?

Kinds and Sources of Information

At this stage, the buyer and the seller must decide what information about the business to seek or give. In the case of Sam's Market, information was brought out about three factors:

1. The nature of the business in the past.
2. Present condition of the business.
3. Relation of the past and present to future expectations.

Bill's approach was proper, but the information he gathered was meager support for decision making.

Some of the information a careful buyer will want may take a lot of money or time to gather. He must decide what sources of information are essential and which ones he can leave untapped. Bill, for instance, might well have inquired about local economic conditions. Full information, it is true, would have required a costly analysis, but consider what information he could have got from easily available sources:

1. Sales in the market had declined more than 50 percent.
2. Sam had been unable to rent commercial space in the building in which the market was located.
3. New supermarkets were operating in the same area.
4. Banks hesitated to gamble on the future of the market.

Bill might also have developed information about the future trend of the business, but that would have required time. He should have known the following facts about his financial program, however:

Available funds		$18,000
Use of funds:		
Payment to Sam	$12,000	
Planned increase in inventory	2,000	
Advertising	500	
Display sign	500	15,000
Available for working capital		$3,000
Expected net income per month (3% of $15,000)		450
Probable expense:		
Payment to bank	$230	
Payment to Sam	240	
Sam's salary	?	

Bill had enough information available to know (1) that his sales expectations were too optimistic and (2) that even if he reached his sales goal, he would not be able to satisfy the cash demand on the operation. What happened could have been predicted.

Analysis

The word "predict" is important. The buyer should be able to follow through the steps listed below and predict with some confidence the future of the business.

What factors affect sales?
> How will these market factors behave?
>> Therefore, what sales can I expect?

What makes up the cost of sales?
> How will these cost factors apply to expected sales?
>> Therefore, what gross profit can I expect?

What expenses are required to run this business?
> How will expenses develop under my ownership?
>> Therefore, what net profit can I predict?

What assets will the business need and possess?
> What is the condition of these assets?
>> Therefore, what asset improvements will I have to make?

What credit does the business assume?
> What is the condition of the credit position?
>> Therefore, what changes, if any, can occur in the debt structure?

How much cash do I have?
> How much cash will the business generate?
>> Therefore, what will be my available-cash position?

What immediate cash outlay must I make?
> What will be the cash needs of the business?
>> Therefore, what cash outgo will be necessary?

What will be my net cash position as things now stand?
> What additional cash resource, if any, must I have?
>> Therefore, what financing plan shall I use?

Value

A business has a purpose. That purpose is to provide a satisfactory return on the owner's investment. Consequently, determining value involves measuring the future profit of the business being sold.

A seller often thinks of value as representing the money he has invested through his years of ownership. A buyer is tempted to consider value as a fair price for tangible items such as equipment and inventory.

These factors are important, but they have value only to the extent that they contribute to future profits. An owner may have invested $20,000, the tangible assets may have a current worth of $10,000, but it is the *profit potential* that establishes the value of the total business.

Assuming that a reliable estimate of future profit is made, how much is to be paid for each dollar of profit potential? This computation is discussed in chapter 6, but the general approach is suggested by the following questions:

What am I buying (or selling)? A business, or a building full of equipment and inventory?

What return would I get if I invested my money elsewhere—in stocks, bonds, or other business opportunities?

What return ought I get from an investment in this business?

Price

It might seem that the price to be paid or received for a business would simply be equal to the value. However, value refers to what a business is worth; price refers to the amount of money for which ownership is transferred. There is usually a difference between price and value because the buyer and seller differ as to how much the business is worth. The price will represent negotiation and compromise. Here are two suggestions for fruitful negotiation:

• Discussion between buyer and seller should focus on the future profit performance of the firm. Since expected profit is basic to determining value, it can be a valuable point for negotiation.

• Every profit projection includes some assumptions and risks. Generally, the less firmly based the assumption and the more apparent the risk, the less value an expected profit can support. Consequently, identifying and analyzing risks involved in future operations can make discussions between buyer and seller more significant.

These two points will help bring negotiations about value toward a mutually acceptable price.

Financing

When the price has been settled, the question of how to finance it remains. Financing a buy-sell transaction involves these five factors:

1. The amount of capital required.
2. The type of capital required.
3. The specific uses to which the capital will be put.
4. The length of time needed to pay back the capital source from the business operation.
5. The sources of available capital.

How much? Bill's failure after buying Sam's Market illustrates a common problem—underestimating the amount of capital required to purchase a business. Capital must be available not only to pay the purchase price but also for (1) funds to operate until the business is generating cash, (2) funds to meet unexpected expenses, and (3) funds as a reserve to allow for errors in expectations. A buyer must think beyond the purchase price to determine the amount of capital he needs. Unless he does he will find his resources embarrassingly and probably disastrously wanting. Here are some questions that must be asked about his capital needs:

Do I have enough capital to pay the purchase price?

Do I have enough capital to support 1 to 3 months' operations—such as payroll and other cash expenses—while the business reaches a self-supporting stage?

Do I have some extra capital to cover needs I may have overlooked (perhaps 10 to 15 percent of the purchase price)?

Types of capital. There are two basic types of capital: (1) equity capital—investment in the business by the owner or owners, and (2) debt capital—borrowed capital that must be repaid.

Equity capital is often called risk capital. Those who furnish the equity capital are expected to take the primary risks of failure and to reap the benefits of success. The equity capital provides a margin of safety for a lender. The greater the amount of equity capital, other things being equal, the easier it is to get debt capital.

The primary source of equity capital is the personal savings of the buyer of the business. Although many small businesses are incorporated, the sale of stock is seldom a source of capital for the small business.

Few buyers, however, have enough personal savings to finance the purchase of a small business without any debt financing. An individual may borrow money for the purchase of a business by obtaining a personal loan, by borrowing against insurance policies, or by refinancing the mortgage on his home. These debts are not direct debts of the business, but the debts of a small business and the personal debts of the owner cannot be completely separated. Banks are the principal institutional source of debt capital for small businesses.

The seller as lender. In the sale and purchase of Sam's Market, the buyer's savings plus a bank loan were not enough to finance the purchase. Bill (who needed more financing) and Sam (who wanted to sell his business) reacted in a manner quite common in the financing of the sale of a small business. Sam agreed to accept payment of part of the purchase price over an extended period of time.

The seller is sometimes a source of capital to the buyer of a small business, as in Bill's case. A happy circumstance if it is handled properly. Before jumping at the chance, however, the buyer should ask himself these questions:

Is there a good reason why commercial lenders would not approve my loan request?

Is the seller so interested in getting out from under the business that he will take an unwise risk?

Am I sure the business is as good as it looks?

Can the business support the debt payments to which I am obligating myself?

In the light of Sam's experience, the seller, too, should pause long enough to answer some questions before he accepts an extended-payment plan.

How serious will it be if the buyer is unable to make his payments?

What security do I have to protect my position?

How capable of operating my business successfully is the buyer?

Contract and Implementation

Every step so far in this discussion has involved forecasting. From motivation to finance, the buyer and the seller must anticipate characteristics, developments, and problems that may develop. The contract between the parties embodies the resulting basic agreements about the business and the relation between buyer and seller. A "good" contract is meaningless if the earlier steps in the process have been carried out carelessly or not at all.

Part 2

Sources of Information
for Buy-Sell Decisions

Chapter 3

Sources of
Market Information

Two BASIC QUESTIONS face the prospective buyer or seller of a small business when he starts to gather information for his decisionmaking:
"What kinds of information do I need?"
"Where can I get this information?"

The information needed can be grouped into three general types: (1) market information, (2) financial information, and (3) legal information. The purpose of this chapter and of chapters 4 and 5 is to identify still further, within these groups, the kinds of information the buyer or seller should look for and some sources of that information. Not all of the sources listed will apply equally to all kinds of businesses. The buyer or seller will have to determine for himself the extent to which the specific types of information will help him reach a sound decision.

Some difficulty may arise in the information-gathering stage because of poor records, unavailability of some information, lack of cooperation, and the like. The seller has the advantage as far as internal data are concerned. He has free access to his own records; the buyer does not. If the buyer needs internal information to reach a decision, it should be made available to him. He should insist on seeing the company records and be wary of any seller who refuses to give him the information he needs.

Either seller or buyer may have to spend considerable time and effort digging out the information. The sources suggested below, however, should help him gather the basic types of information needed in the decisionmaking process.

Importance of Market Information

The first and most logical step in buying or selling a business is to conduct a market analysis. A market analysis is a study of the present position of the business within its market area and of probable future patterns. It should include the growth pattern of the business being sold, the state of the market, the nature and extent of competition—all factors, in fact, that will show the present market position of the business or that will affect its future.

A market analysis should indicate whether the purchase or sale of the business should be considered further. It will help the *seller* decide what valuation to place on the business for sale purposes. It will help the *buyer* decide how much he should pay, and it will also give him a clearer picture of just what he is buying. A market analysis has the added value of making it possible to develop more accurate sales forecasts. It places greater emphasis on fact and less on hunch and guesswork.

The specific nature of the business being bought or sold will determine much of the market information needed. A manufacturing business with problems of marketing and distribution will need information not necessarily pertinent to a retail or service business, with its more localized market. The following areas of market information are designed to suggest sources that may be useful to the buyer or the seller in analyzing the market of the business.

Sales Information

An investigation should be made of the sales history of the company. At least 3 years' sales should be examined and preferably 10 years'—or the entire sales history of the company if it is a new one.

The manner in which the records are kept will determine to a large extent the availability of sales information. Many small businesses keep little in the way of sales records—often only what is necessary for tax purposes. Others have bookkeeping systems designed by business-machine manufacturers, trade associations, or professional accounting services. The more standardized the procedure, the more useful the information is likely to be for market analysis.

Most States now have sales taxes, and this may provide a useful source of information. Whether or not a business is required to keep sales-tax records depends largely on the type of business and the State requirements. Sales-tax laws are not uniform, and what is required in one State may not be required in another.

If most of the business is done on a credit basis, accounts receivable may give useful sales information. If this source is used, the market investigation should be concerned only with the amount of credit sales and not with the effectiveness of the collection of accounts receivable.

Ingenuity and common sense can often turn up sources of sales information. In one case, for example, sales for a self-service laundry were determined by using water capacity per machine, city records of the amount of water consumed by the business, and price per load.

Regardless of where the sales information comes from, the purpose of gathering it is basically the same—to identify the pattern or trend of sales over the past and to use this information to project or estimate sales for the period ahead. Such an investigation is especially useful in determining the value of the business above the value of the assets.

Cost of Goods Sold

A study of the cost of goods sold is also important in determining the market position of the business. Cost of goods sold is the cost of merchandise purchased by the business for resale, including freight and other charges. The difference between sales and the cost of the goods sold is called *gross margin* or *gross profit*. The higher the cost of goods sold in relation to sales, the lower the gross margin—and the net profit.

Many factors, both within the company and in the market of which the business is a part, affect the cost of goods sold. An investigation should be made to determine the following:

1. *Average rate of stock turnover,* particularly as compared to the normal or typical rate for similar businesses.
2. *Extent to which invoices are being discounted.* Paying invoices in time to earn the cash discount will increase both gross margin and net profit if the discount is recorded as a reduction in the cost of goods sold. A direct increase in net profit will result if the discount is shown as "other income."
3. *Freight costs* to determine whether incoming transportation charges are in line.

Among the records to be studied are vendor invoices, records of merchandise payments to vendors, shipper receipts or bills of lading, and records of past physical inventories.

Sales-Effort Records

This information has to do with how much it costs in selling effort to produce a given volume of sales. It involves two types of costs: (1) advertising costs, from invoices and statements for various forms of advertising and promotion; and (2) salaries and wages paid for selling, from payroll or Social Security records. If the business maintains salespeople in the field, as a manufacturer might, information on reimbursable travel expenses should be included.

The purpose of gathering information on selling costs is to determine how well these costs are being utilized and to compare them with average figures for the kind of business being studied.

Personal Observation

Personal observation of the premises and personnel of the company is another source of information for the buy-sell process. Just what points should be noted will depend on the nature of the business, but the following are offered as examples:

The general appearance of the premises, both internal and external, may be important, particularly if direct customer contact is made at the place of business.

Plant layout and apparent efficiency of operation should be carefully observed if the seller is a manufacturer or otherwise engaged in processing or assembly.

Employee morale and general attitude toward the business should be noted, especially if current employees are to be retained.

Employee records, including wage-payment plans, employee-evaluation and merit-rating programs, training programs, and so on should be studied.

Market Information From Outside Sources

Sources of market information outside the business fall into two general classes: (1) competing businesses, and (2) the total market of the business and the factors that enter into it. Analyzing market characteristics involves dealing with constantly changing forces. This is in contrast to the internal analysis, which concerns basically historical records.

Competition. Unless the business has a monopoly of some sort, a study of the competition should be included in the market analysis. The competition may be local and well defined, or quite generalized, depending on the nature of the business and of the market.

Trade associations and other data-gathering agencies, both governmental and nongovernmental, are sometimes helpful in this area. A good deal of the information about competition, however, must come from direct investigation, business by business.

Such factors as these are of interest: estimated sales, advertising and promotion, services offered, performance of sales personnel, businesses entering and leaving the competition recently, changes in the competitive structure through product mix or services offered, pricing policies, and other factors that form a part of the competitive patterns for specific types of businesses. A very important aspect of competition is the extent to which the total weight of competition has expanded the market for certain types of products or kinds of businesses, and the direction this is taking.

Location. In certain businesses, location may not be too important, providing the physical plant is structurally sound and suitable for the business. In other cases, location may be a vital factor. An important point that should be looked into is the status of the location and any plans for proposed changes that may have an adverse effect on the future of the business. Urban renewal programs are causing many small businesses to look for new locations. So are changes in highways and streets, flood-control programs, changes in zoning ordinances, and the like.

The buyer, whether he will own the physical plant or lease it, should look into the possibility of future expansion. Consulting a competent architect or engineer now may save trouble later on if the buyer should want to expand and leasing provisions allow him to.

Population and purchasing power. The number of people within the market area and the amount of spendable income they have are important market factors. For many kinds of businesses, the total population is less important than certain segments of the population. A business selling hearing aids, for example, will be interested only in persons who have hearing difficulties.

In gathering information on income and expenditures, three factors should be kept in mind: (1) the total purchasing power based on total population; (2) the average or median income for the typical family unit; (3) the amount or percent of expenditures for various types of goods and services.

General population figures are obtained from Federal, State, and local government sources. The Federal census, taken every 10 years, gives not only total population figures but also breakdowns that are useful in many business situations. For most of the larger cities, census figures are further classified by sections within the city on the basis of certain population and economic characteristics. These sections are called census tracts.

Business population figures may be available from numerous sources. The Yellow Pages of the telephone directory and the city directory are local sources that are immediately available. Chambers of commerce, trade associations, and State and Federal government agencies can often be helpful.

The 10-year census reports the income for 20 percent of the total population on a National, State, county, city, and census-tract basis. Other information issued by the Department of Commerce can also be useful.

Many trade associations report the results of research on consumer expenditures. Other sources of data on income include the following: (1) planning commission offices, (2) employment offices, (3) research done by newspapers, (4) building permits, especially in newly developed areas, and (5) mortgage and loan companies. Numerous fact-gathering agencies develop and publish estimates of consumer income and expenditures for various classes of goods and services.

General market conditions. A much broader yet vital part of the market analysis has to do with what might be called the general state of the market. Most of the discussion of market analysis so far has dealt with factors that have a direct influence on the business being bought or sold: company sales, location, competition, and so on. But these, in turn, are influenced by the overall economic conditions of the country and of the market area. These may be widespread movements such as national cycles of prosperity and depression, or they may be purely local conditions. The two extremes are not necessarily related.

It is to the advantage of the buyer or seller to have a clear understanding of economic factors that affect or are likely to affect the status of the business. The significance of this information becomes clearer when forecasts and estimates are made.

Some questions to be used as a guide in market analysis are given in chapter 12.

Chapter 4

Sources of
Financial Information

BOTH BUYER AND SELLER are interested in financial information affecting the buy-sell transaction. However, since the seller already has this information, it is a major requirement for the buyer to get and make use of as much of it as possible.

The buyer can usually find financial information in the following places: (1) financial statements, (2) income-tax returns, (3) other internal records, and (4) other external sources.

Financial Statements

The results of the financial transactions of every company *should* be reflected in its periodic financial statements. These statements are extremely important in buying or selling a small business. They were prepared for the seller, of course, and their contents are available to him. But the buyer, too, should be aware during the early stages of a buy-sell transaction of the information contained in financial statements.

Balance sheet and income statement. The balance sheet is a statement of the financial position of the business at a given moment in time. The income statement is a summary of the revenue and expenses of the business during a specified period of time. These financial statements show only the past results of the company's transactions. The results of future operations may or may not be similar.

Balance sheets and income statements in themselves contain important information, but they are most useful when a professional accountant makes a detailed analysis of them. A complete analysis includes a review of the manner in which the statements were prepared, and perhaps also a review of the records and control features of the accounting system. This is especially important in a small business buy-sell transaction because the financial statements of smaller companies are not usually as professionally prepared as the statements for larger companies. An accountant should be brought into the buy-sell transaction as early as possible by the seller as well as by the buyer.

Audited statements. In many buy-sell transactions, the statements are supplied by the seller, but the buyer reserves the right to conduct an audit of the seller's records. Or the buyer insists that the seller "warrant" his financial statements. Warranty of financial statements by the seller should be accepted with caution, however, because there does not seem to be any uniform definition of the term warranty.

If the seller's financial statements are prepared by an independent accountant, the statements should show whether they were (1) prepared after an audit of the seller's accounts, or (2) prepared from the seller's records without verification by audit. If they were prepared without verification by audit, they may be quite similar or even identical to statements that would have been prepared by the seller's own book-keeper. If they were prepared after an audit, they should include a statement of the accountant's opinion.

Financial statements prepared without such an audit may or may not reflect the financial position or results of operation of the company. Most small companies do not have their records audited annually, but without an audit it is impossible to tell how accurate the statements really are.

Other considerations. The buyer should request balance sheets and income statements for at least 3 and preferably 10 years. If the seller is a new company, financial statements for the entire life of the company should be requested.

Other financial statements are sometimes available to the buyer. These include such items as statements of cost of goods manufactured (if the seller is a manufacturer), application of funds, and variances from the budget.

Another point the buyer should consider is the cutoff period for the financial statements. The statements may have been cut off during the low period of the sales cycle or during the high period. This has some bearing on the financial position reflected in the statements.

More detailed information on financial statements and their analysis is given in chapters 9, 10, and 11.

Income-Tax Returns

If independent accountants did not prepare the financial statements, the seller may or may not have complete sets of statements. He should have at least an annual income statement—that much is required for income-tax purposes. If the seller is a partnership or corporation, the tax returns should have balance sheets attached. If the seller is a sole proprietorship, tax returns will not show balance-sheet data.

Financial statements prepared for income-tax purposes may be very different from statements prepared in conformity with generally accepted accounting principles. Those prepared for tax returns are designed to present the desired tax position in compliance with the income-tax laws. Financial statements for nontax purposes have different objectives and therefore may reflect different financial information.

Many small companies prepare financial statements only for income-tax purposes and use those statements for all management decisions. This may or may not give the desired results. The parties to a buy-sell transaction are interested in statements reflecting the tax position, but they should concern themselves also with statements reflecting nontax items.

The buyer should request copies of tax returns for at least 3 and preferably 10 years or, if the seller is a new company, for the life of the company. The tax returns are more important in buying the stock of a corporation than in buying the assets of a corporation, partnership, or sole proprietorship.

The corporation is an income-tax entity; the partnership and sole proprietorship are not. A partnership is required to file income-tax information returns but does not pay income taxes as a company—the taxable income is passed on to the partners, and they pay the tax as individuals. No tax return is filed for a sole proprietorship, but the income statement is included as a part of the sole proprietor's personal income-tax return.

The buyer should find out which tax returns have been examined by the Internal Revenue Service and which have not. This is particularly important if the buyer is purchasing the stock of a corporation. If a corporation with an operating loss is being acquired, the loss might have value and the buyer should satisfy himself as to whether this net operating loss can be utilized. In many instances, the only information available to the buyer is that found with the income-tax returns.

Other Internal Sources

The financial statements are usually supported by detailed analyses of selected accounts. This might include some of the following items: Sales may have been analyzed by customer, product, division, salesman, time period, and any other classifications necessary.

Purchases may be classified according to product, time period, territory, supplier, or other classification.

If the seller is a manufacturer, he may have cost-control reports that include analyses of material costs, labor costs, overhead cost, scrap sales, spoiled and defective goods, and other items.

There may be a cash-flow statement—perhaps incorporated with the analysis of collections of accounts receivable—and even a projection of cash requirements.

The seller may have a regular budgeting program with projections into the near or distant future. It is common practice for the buyer to require the seller to make a projection for at least a year from the date of the proposed transfer. The buyer should insist on this projection.

Other External Sources

The seller's suppliers are an excellent source of information for the buyer. They can provide records showing the volume of purchases by the seller. This information may be difficult to get in some cases, particularly if the seller informs his suppliers that it is proprietary information.

Another source of data is the seller's banker. A banker can supply information about cash position, line of credit, and other fiscal data. He may, however, be ruluctant to release this information.

The seller may have filed payroll-tax reports, sales-tax reports, excise-tax reports, ICC reports, or any of many other government reports. Some of this information is available to a buyer.

The buyer may seek information about the seller from credit agencies or credit associations related to trade associations. Usually, the buyer must have a contact with these agencies in order to get the information, but there are many ways to get reports about the seller.

A number of organizations, including trade associations, supply information about industry averages. These averages are very important to the buyer for judging the effectiveness of the seller.

Advice to the Seller

The seller, for his part, should be cautious about releasing information to the buyer. It is entirely possible that the supposed buyer is a competitor, or may be one in the future. Often a seller is so anxious to sell that he supplies any information requested by the buyer without even getting a good-faith deposit. He may spend many dollars in collecting the data for the buyer. A seller should not supply any information to anyone without first discussing the matter with his accountant and his attorney.

Chapter 5

Sources of
Legal Information

THE PROSPECTIVE BUYER OF A BUSINESS can play an important role in the discovery of legal problems that may affect the value of the business and his decision on whether to buy. Legal opinions are the responsibility of the buyer's attorney, of course. But the attorney must often rely on the buyer as his source of internal information about the business—information he will need in making his legal recommendations. It is therefore important that the buyer have some idea as to what his attorney will expect of him.

As in any sale, the basic legal problem in the purchase of a business involves the transfer of ownership or title to property. How serious the title problem is varies from one business to another, depending on the nature of the assets being purchased.

If the transaction involved only the transfer of good title to a single piece of real estate, it would be a simple matter. But buying and selling a business typically involves a conglomeration of assets—inventory, fixtures, vehicles, and equipment, all of which are movable, and assorted contract rights under leases, sales agreements, patent licenses, and so on, which are intangible.

Each asset has its own ownership aspects. It is important to ask this question about each asset: "Is the buyer getting the ownership rights he assumes he is getting?"

An even more careful investigation from a legal point of view is called for when the buyer either assumes liabilities or purchases the

27

stock of a corporation. Even the risk of potential liabilities—liabilities that may occur in the future because of past events—may be reduced by proper investigation.

Both internal and external sources of legal information are usually available to the buyer and his attorney for examination. The buyer should not rely solely on the oral statements of the seller as to important aspects of the business. Any statements of the seller that have to be accepted without support from other sources should be incorporated into the buy-sell contract as warranties.

How much information should a buyer obtain about a business before legally committing himself to purchase? There is no easy answer to this question, but the buyer should realize that the legal risk he assumes is about inversely proportional to the amount of information he has obtained about the business.

Internal Sources of Legal Information

Among the internal sources of legal information are copies of contracts, evidences of ownership, and organizational documents. Personally examining the business premises and questioning the seller and his employees may be the only source of information about some assets.

Contracts. The buyer and seller are both concerned with the rights and obligations created by outstanding contracts with suppliers, customers, creditors, employees, lessors, and so on. The seller is concerned with his liability for any breach of contract that may result from sale of the business. He should know that ordinarily only contract rights, and not contract obligations, may be transferred to a third party without the consent of the other party to the original contract. Sublease arrangements and mortgage assumptions are examples of this. The seller remains liable even though the buyer takes over the lease or mortgage as part of the buy-sell contract.

Here is an example involving a lease. A food merchant sold one of his smaller stores at what he considered a good profit. The sale price covered inventory, fixtures, and goodwill, for which the seller received $28,000. He had purchased the business 2 years before for $15,000.

The building was leased, and the seller was not able to assign the lease to the new owner of the business. He was, however, permitted to sublease the building for the remainder of the lease. The lease amounted to $650 a month.

Recently, sales have been decreasing to the point where the present owner has threatened to give up the business and take his loss. If he should do so, the former owner will be liable for the remaining 2 years' lease. Unless he can find another tenant, he may lose all he gained from the sale and more.

Assignment of contracts. The buyer often wants any contractual rights of the seller that are needed in order to maintain the business as a going concern. In legal terminology, the transfer of contractual rights is called an assignment. Generally, a contractual right is assignable, but the original contract may expressly prohibit its assignment.

Such negative provisions are common in printed forms of leases. Loan agreements may prohibit the sale or other change in ownership of substantially all the business assets. Or they may call for speeding up payment of the principal if the assets do change hands. The buyer should get copies of important contracts and review them to determine whether they have nonassignment clauses.

A contract may be nonassignable, however, even without such a provision. This would be true if the contract rights are coupled with obligations of a personal character. For example, the seller's credit arrangements with a supplier are not assignable because they are based on the seller's reputation as a credit risk. A contract for the manufacture of certain goods may not be assignable because the customer, when he signed the contract, knew and was relying on the superior workmanship of the seller. Likewise, a supplier's agreement to supply the seller's manufacturing requirements of certain raw materials may not be assignable because the requirements of the new owner are uncertain.

Both buyer and seller should remember that third parties will, in all probability, have to be reckoned with in carrying out the buy-sell transaction. If the buyer must have a contract that is nonassignable and the seller is not a corporation, the only solution is to renegotiate the contract. In the case of a corporate seller, it may be possible to make the transaction a purchase of stock rather than assets.

Types of contracts. Following are some recommendations to the buyer about specific types of contracts:

Copies of real-estate leases should be obtained from the seller and examined for provisions relating to amount of rent, terms of payment, expiration, renewal, subleasing, repair, improvement, insurance, and so on. The buyer should pay special attention to the duration of the lease. If the term remaining is too short, either the lease should be renegotiated *before the purchase* or an option should be obtained to renew for an additional period. Leases for a specific term are often misleading because of provisions granting to one or both of the parties the right to terminate the lease by giving a stated period of notice.

Copies of patent, trademark, trade-name, and copyright registrations should be obtained in order to determine the legal status of the right and whether it can be transferred.

The principle subject of the buy-sell transaction may be a *contract right to be the exclusive agent, dealer or distributor* of a product or line of products, or the right under license to use a patented process, trade name, or trademark. Copies of such contracts should be obtained to determine the precise nature of the right, its limitations, and the seller's power to transfer. Particular attention should be given to the exclusiveness of the right.

Copies of employment contracts and union agreements should be studied for terms relating to compensation, working conditions, duration of employment, termination, pension and profit-sharing plans, stock option, insurance programs, and so on. The buyer should find out whether key employees will remain with the company if the ownership changes hands. If the employees have not been organized, he should inquire about possible activities of union organizers among them.

The buyer should study *outstanding sale and purchase contracts.* Particular attention should be given to trade-credit, discount, installament-payment, and security requirements. The buyer should get from the seller copies of conditional-sale contracts, purchase-money chattel mortgages, chattel leases, lease-purchase agreements, consignment contracts, and sale-on-approval and sale-or-return contracts to which the seller is a party.

The buyer should also get from the seller copies of *financing agreements* between the seller and commercial banks, finance companies, and other third-party lenders. Attention should be given to the term of the loan, repayment provisions, interest rate, finance charges, insurance requirements, acceleration provisions, security requirements, and recourse rights. The buyer will generally have to make his own financing arrangements, but the seller's experience in financing the business will often suggest what the buyer can expect if he purchases the business.

A buyer's willingness to purchase *accounts receivable,* apart from his financial ability to do so, should depend on their apparent collectibility. The buyer should require the seller to submit a complete list according to the age of the accounts. Inquiry may disclose factors other than the statute of limitations that would prevent collection.

A study of the seller's *insurance policies* may give the buyer some insight into the availability, adequacy, and cost of coverage of such risks as liability arising from manufacture or sale of defective products, liability to customers for injuries sustained on the premises, liability for property damage and bodily injury arising from negligent operation of company vehicles, liability to employees for injury under workmen's compensation laws, and property hazards such as fire, windstorm, and theft. The buyer should be aware, however, that premium rates based on the seller's experience may not be available to him.

Evidences of Ownership. The buyer should get from the seller a certified abstract of title for each parcel of real estate involved in the transaction. The abstract should be examined by the buyer's attorney.

In addition to disclosing any defects in the title, examination of the abstract and the abstractor's certificate will usually show whether there are any unreleased mortgages, judgment liens, mechanics' liens, tax liens, or unpaid real-estate taxes and special assessments.

The seller should be asked to show evidence of his ownership of principal items of personal property in the form of bills of sales, receipts, assignments, motor-vehicle title certificates, and so on. Such evidence will not prove that there are no recorded liens against the property, but lack of it should alert the buyer to the possibility that personal property in the physical possession of the seller is rented, leased, borrowed, or delivered on consignment.

Organizational documents. If the seller is a partnership, the buyer should get a copy of the partnership agreement. If there is no written agreement, he should find out who the partners are and whether authority exists to sell the business assets.

If the seller is a corporation, the buyer should get a certified copy of the resolution of the shareholders authorizing the sale of the corporate assets. In a corporation stock transaction, he should get a copy of all organizational documents. These documents include the articles of incorporation and amendments to it, the corporate bylaws, stock-transfer books, and minutes of shareholders' and directors' meetings.

Observation and inquiry. Certain types of legal problems can be uncovered only by observation and inquiry. This is true of mechanics' liens. The basis for mechanics' liens against real estate may exist even though no lien is on file. If the buyer learns that there has been repair or construction within the allowable period for filing mechanics' liens, he should check with the contractors and suppliers to find out whether they have been paid.

The real estate should be examined to make sure that it complies with building codes and other ordinances. It is advisable also to have the real estate surveyed to determine whether buildings are located within boundaries in compliance with setback lines, whether adjoining buildings or driveways are encroaching upon the property, and so on.

External Sources of Legal Information

Among the more common external sources of legal information are public records, government agencies, and third parties with whom the seller has had dealings.

Office of record. A down-to-date abstract of title will ordinarily disclose the existence of liens against a particular panel of real estate, but liens against personal property of the seller can be discovered only by a search of the office of record. Separate filing systems may exist for chattel mortgages, conditional sales contracts, trust receipts, assignment of accounts receivable, and so on. Each of these files must be checked.

A record search will not disclose what items of personal property in possession of the seller have been rented, leased, borrowed, or delivered on consignment. Also, lien notations on motor-vehicle title certificates may take precedence over recording—it depends on State statutes.

Tax authorities. Investigation is especially important where the buyer is purchasing the stock of the seller or assuming liability for the payment status of Federal, State, and local income taxes, Social Security and income-withholding taxes, Federal excise taxes, State and local taxes, license taxes, and real- and personal-property taxes. Have tax returns been reviewed and approved by the taxing authority?

Zoning ordinances, planning agencies, building codes. The buyer should check zoning ordinances and building codes to determine the existence of nonconforming land uses or violations of building codes Comprehensive zoning plans may provide for steps to be taken toward elimination of nonconforming uses. This can be done by prohibiting alteration or enlarging of buildings or by requiring liquidation of nonconforming use within a prescribed period of time.

City, county, or metropolitan planning agencies and engineering departments should be consulted about the existence of master plans for future rezoning, redevelopment, and street or highway changes. Highway relocation, limited street or highway access, elimination of on-street parking, or changes in the composition of the immediate market area may be enough to destroy the business as a going concern. City annexation policies may be important to businesses located in the suburbs. The cost of planned improvements may affect the buyer's decision.

Court records. The buyer should find out from court records whether judgment liens exist against real estate involved in the buy-sell transaction and whether lawsuits are pending that may retroactively result in the attachment of liens. This is of particular concern to the buyer who either assumes business liabilities or purchases the stock of a corporation. Not only litigation costs and liability must be considered but also the impact of the publicity on the goodwill of the business.

Even if a court record search is negative, future litigation may arise out of events of the past several years, such as motor-vehicle accidents, manufacture or sale of defective products, accidents on the premises involving customers or employees, breach of contract, violations of wage-and-hour laws, and so on. The best protection is to inquire of the seller and of employees who have been intimately concerned with the business.

Part 3

The Buy-Sell Process

Chapter 6

Determining the Value of a Business

Tʜᴇ ᴍᴏsᴛ ᴅɪꜰꜰɪᴄᴜʟᴛ sᴛᴇᴘ in buying or selling a small business is probably determining what the business is worth as a going concern. Many judgment decisions must be made. Yet before negotiations can continue successfully, a value must be established. The value must be acceptable to both buyer and seller, or further negotiation is fruitless. It must result from the logical and objective efforts of all the parties involved.

Valuation Methods

There are two basic methods of determining the value of a business. The first is based on expectations of future profits and return on investment. This method is preferable by far. It forces the buyer and seller to give at least minimum attention to such factors as trends in sales and profits, capitalized value of the business, and expectancy of return on investment.

The second method is based on the appraised value of the assets at the time of negotiation. It assumes that these assets will continue to be used in the business. This method gives little consideration to the future of the business. It determines asset values only as they relate to the present. It is the more commonly used, not because it is more reliable, but because it is easier. The projections needed to value the business on the basis of future profits are difficult to make.

Looking Ahead

Whichever method is to be used to value the business, the buyer should ask the seller to prepare a pro forma, or projected, statement of income and profit or loss for at least the next 12 months. For this, the seller will prepare a sales estimate for this period along with a matching estimate of the cost of goods sold and operating expense.

The projected statement will reflect the net profit the seller believes possible. The buyer should then make his own estimate of sales, cost of goods sold, operating expenses, and net profit for the next year at least, and as far into the future as possible.

In preparing these statements, the buyer should start by analyzing the actual statements of profit and loss for at least 5 years back. He should be sure that the past and projected statements provided by the seller are correct and are consistent with the buyer's proposed future operation. He should also study general and local economic changes that will affect future business. This includes competition.

If the buyer is not qualified to prepare projected financial statements, he should consult an independent accountant. This will involve some expense, but the cost will be small compared to the loss he might incur if he invested in a small business with a doubtful future.

Financial statements and their analysis are discussed in part 4; market analysis in part 5.

Forecasting Sales

The most important projection to be determined in the projected income statement is the sales figure. After this number has been established, the cost, expense, and profit figures are easier to acquire. The data for projecting sales will come from past sales records of the business. The more accurate and systematic these records are, the more confidently they can be used in estimating future sales.

How long a forecast? A basic question is this: "Over how long a period of time is it necessary or possible to forecast sales?" Any forecast is uncertain, and the farther a forecast is projected into the future, the greater the uncertainty. While it may be possible to exercise at least reasonable control over the internal operation, the external economic and market factors make forecasting difficult because of lack of control.

Perhaps the best way to approach the length of the forecast is in terms of the expected return on investment. Suppose it is estimated that the business should bring a 20 percent return on initial investment. The investment, then, should be returned in 5 years. At this point, the owner would just break even on his original investment. It seems logical to project sales and profits over a span of time comparable to that estimated for return on investment—in the above illustration, 5 years.

Any such forecast, however, should give careful consideration to expected changes either in the economy or in the industry market that might affect the pattern of sales change. Mathematically, it is possible to forecast sales with some precision. Realistically, however, this precision is dulled because vital market and economic factors cannot be controlled.

Methods of forecasting sales. There are numerous methods by which sales forecasts can be made. Most of them take their lead from the past sales performance of the company. For establishing trends or averages, 5 years of sales history is better than 3, and 10 is better than 5.

Perhaps the simplest method is to assume that the percentage increase (or decrease) in sales will continue and that no market factors will influence sales performance more in the future than in the past. Suppose, for example, that the rate of yearly average increase for the past 5 years has been 4 percent, and that each year has shown about this rate of increase. Then it might be assumed that sales for the next year will be 4 percent greater than the current or most recent year.

But what about the year following? The year after that? Can it be assumed that these years will also increase at about 4-percent level? Each additional year into the future reduces the certainty of the predictions.

If these negative influences limit the accuracy to such an extent, why try to forecast beyond the immediate future (1 year)? Because such a forecast forces the person making it to give at least a little attention to economic and market factors that might influence the future operation—that might, in fact, indicate that the purchase or sale of the business would not be wise.

With forecasts covering more than 1 or 2 years, a more detailed forecasting technique is needed. Such technique should be designed to weight out extreme variations in year-to-year sales and to give a trend or level of sales change that is more realistically oriented to probable future sales patterns.

No method of forecasting can set any value on external market conditions, because there is no guarantee that these conditions will carry over into the future with the same relative significance. Nevertheless, their possible influence should be considered.

Some simple methods of short-term forecasting are described in chapter 14.

Risk and Return on Investment

If a buyer wants to invest money in a business that is being sold, he should be concerned about receiving a fair return on his investment.

Many businesses can make a profit for a short time (1 to 5 years); not so many operate profitably over a longer period of time.

From the buyer's point of view, what is a fair rate of return from an investment in a small business? The rate of return is usually related to the risk factor—the higher the risk, the higher the return should be. United States Government bonds are the safest investment—the rate of return ranges from 5½ to 6 percent. Blue-chip stocks and corporate bonds usually give the investor a return of 4 to 10 percent if both dividends or interest and increase in market value are considered. Speculative stocks may have a higher return, but they also have a higher risk factor.

The buyer of a small business should try to determine the risk factor of the new business, though this is difficult at best and in many cases impossible. In attempting to assess the risk factor, the buyer should project the profits of the business as far into the future as possible. He should ask himself how high the risk should be normally and look for conditions that would be likely to affect the sales and profitmaking capability of the business.

In any event, he should consider carefully the minimum return on investment that *he* is willing to accept. This concept of risk is important in valuing the business by capitalization of future earnings.

Valuing the Business by Capitalizing Future Earnings

The price to be paid by the buyer should be based on the capitalized value of future earnings. Instead, however, in most small business buy-sell transactions, price is based on the purchase and sale of assets. Profits are made by utilizing assets, of course, but actually the assets purchased are only incidental to the future profits of the new business.

Capitalized value is the capital value that would bring the stated earnings at a specified rate of interest. The rate used is usually the current rate of return for investments involving a similar amount of risk. The capitalized value is found by dividing the annual profit by the specified rate of return expressed as a decimal.

Assume for the moment that the future profits of a business have been projected for the next 5 years and are estimated to average $10,000 a year. (This is in addition to compensation for the services of the buyer and any members of his family.) What should be the sales price for the buy-sell transaction?

If this investment were as safe as U.S. Government bonds, the buyer should be willing to pay $167,000 ($10,000÷.06). If the investment is considered as safe as an investment in an excellent corporate stock that earns 10 percent in dividends and price increases, the buyer should be willing to pay $100,000 ($10,000÷.10).

Very few small businesses, however, have as low a risk factor as these two investments. What rate, then, should be used in capitalizing the earnings of a small business? Usually, 20 to 25 percent is considered adequate. This means that the buyer should pay between $40,000 and $50,000 for this business. If it earns the projected $10,000 a year, the buyer will recover his initial investment in 4 or 5 years. This time will be extended by Federal and State income taxes to be paid on the income, but this would also be the case for most alternative investments except nontaxable municipal securities.

In using a computation such as this, the importance of long-run profits should be kept in mind. Unless profits are possible over a long period of time (10 to 15 years), investment in a small business may be a poor decision. The trend of profits is also important. If all other factors are the same, a company whose profits are declining is worth less than one whose profits are increasing.

Valuing the Business on the Basis of Asset Appraisal

The majority of buy-sell transactions are based on a value established for the assets of the company. This approach is not recommended, but if it is to be used, the suggestions that follow should be considered.

A most important point is to find out early in the transaction just what assets are to be transferred. Usually, the seller has some personal items that he does not wish to sell. Prepaid insurance, some supplies and the like, in addition to cash, marketable securities, accounts receivable, and notes receivable usually are not sold. If the buyer does purchase the receivables, the seller may guarantee their collection, but such a guarantee should be established.

The assets most commonly purchased in a small business buy-sell transaction are merchandise inventory, sales and office supplies, fixtures and equipment, and goodwill.

Evaluating goodwill. One of the assets that must be considered in a buy-sell transaction is goodwill. Goodwill, in a general sense, arises from all the special advantages connected with a going concern—its good name, capable staff and personnel, high financial standing, reputation for superior products and customer services, and favorable location.

From the accounting point of view, goodwill is the ability of a business to realize above-normal profits as a result of these factors. By above-normal profit is meant a higher rate of return on the investment than that ordinarily necessary to attract investors to that type of business.

The value of goodwill can be computed in either of the following ways:

1. *Capitalization of average net earnings.* As explained above, the amount to be paid for a business may be determined by capitalizing

expected future earnings at a rate that represents the required return on investment. The difference between this amount and the appraised value of the physical assets may be considered the price of goodwill.

This method uses only earnings in computing the price to be paid for the business. For that part of the calculation, it ignores the appraised value of the assets.

2. *Capitalization of average excess earnings.* This method recognizes both earnings and asset contributions. It starts with the appraised value of the assets and computes what would be a fair return on that value. If the estimated future earnings are higher than this "fair return," the difference between the two figures—the "excess earnings"—is capitalized at a higher rate, and the amount thus obtained is considered the goodwill value. This figure is added to the appraised value of the assets to give a price for the business.

Payment of excess earnings is often stated in terms of "years of purchase" instead of in terms of capitalization at a certain interest rate. Capitalization of average earnings at 20 percent is the same as payment for 5 years' excess earnings.

As the above discussion shows, the determination of goodwill usually reflects the value of profits that will be realized by the buyer above the normal rate of return; that is, the excess profits. But most small businesses that are for sale do not have excess profits. They usually show nominal profits or none at all. Often the seller makes an offer that seems quite good, but the buyer must be able to eliminate the seller's emotions and reduce all facts to workable relationships.

If there are excess profits, goodwill is usually valued by capitalizing them at a fixed percentage established by bargaining between the seller and the buyer. The capitalization percentage needs to be high because profits higher than a normal return are difficult to maintain. Excess profits of $2,000 capitalized at 10 percent will give a goodwill value of $20,000 ($2,000÷.10). Capitalizing the same excess profits at 20 percent gives a goodwill value of $10,000 ($2,000÷.20).

Although goodwill valuation is the first asset valuation to be discussed here, it is normally the last to be computed. Since few small businesses being sold are producing excess profits, the problem of goodwill value is not a pressing one in most buy-sell transactions.

Merchandise inventory. In a service business, placing a value on the inventories is a minor problem; but in distributive and manufacturing businesses, the inventory is likely to be the largest single asset. A manufacturer, for example, has three inventories—raw material, work in process, and finished goods—and each of them presents different problems in valuation. The distributive company has only one inventory, called merchandise inventory.

The financial statements presented by the seller will probably reflect an inventory value different from the one assigned in a buy-sell transaction. Inventories are usually carried on the books either at cost or at the lower of cost or market. Market is defined as the current replacement cost to the seller.

In determining the value of inventories, the seller has to choose a method of arriving at cost. The most common costing methods are first-in-first-out (FIFO), last-in-first-out (LIFO), and average cost. These methods may give very different values and the buyer and seller must arrive at some value agreeable to both. The most common methods used in valuing inventories for buying and selling small businesses are cost of last purchase and current market price.

The quantity of the inventory is usually determined by a physical count. The physical inventory procedures should be decided before the count, and each inventory team should include one representative from the buyer and one from the seller. It is easy to omit items from the inventory count, and here the seller is usually in a more vulnerable position than the buyer. There is more danger of omitting items from the count than of double counting them.

It may be that some items of inventory are not to be sold. If so, these items should be segregated before the count begins. Another problem is determining what quality of items are to be included in the inventory. The buyer needs to be cautious when examining the inventories—in most buy-sell situations there is some inventory that is not salable.

This is one reason why the buyer should employ as his representatives on the inventory teams individuals who are acquainted with that type of inventory. If the buyer and the seller disagree on the value of certain items, the seller will remove these items from the list of inventory for sale.

When the inventory is being priced, be very careful in matching price to quantity. Be sure that the units in which the quantity is recorded and the units priced are the same. The physical count should be recorded in duplicate so that buyer and seller can each make separate extensions after all prices have been listed. After independent extensions, the two inventories should be reconciled.

Manufacturer's inventory. When a manufacturing company is being exchanged, the raw materials inventory is taken and priced like the merchandise inventory of a distributive business. The work-in-process and finished-goods inventories may present a problem. Usually, there is no market price or cost of last purchase to relate to these inventories; consequently, the seller's cost is generally used for establishing prices.

If the seller has unused plant capacity or if his plant is inefficient, his costs may be inflated. Such a situation requires the help of an accountant with a good knowledge of cost accounting.

41

Store supplies and office supplies. These two items are usually quite small. They should present no problem, though some of them may have no value to the buyer if the name of the company is to be changed. After the usable supplies have been determined, a physical inventory should be taken and priced as in the case of the merchandise inventory.

Property assets and accumulated depreciation. The property-asset account normally reflects the cost of the assets reduced by a provision for depreciation. In many small business buy-sell transactions, no real property is exchanged, because the plant site is leased. The problem of establishing a value on real estate is not as acute, anyway, since the market value for real property does not fluctuate as widely as the market value for personal property.

It is customary to have an independent appraiser establish a value for real property. Appraisers' findings on real property are usually more acceptable to both parties than personal-property appraisals— the real property may have multiple uses, whereas personal property consists of single-purpose assets. The book value of real property will be close to the appraisal value unless the property has been held for a long period of time or unusual circumstances have caused sudden and drastic changes of real-property values.

Personal-property assets. The buyer may feel that he knows going values of the personal property and decide not to retain an independent appraiser. In addition, many individuals believe that cost or book value is a good place to begin negotiations for personal property. However, because of the many methods of computing depreciation and also because of conflicting ideas about capitalizing costs, the cost or book value may not reflect a value that is agreeable to both parties.

It is difficult to assign a value to personal property equipment because these assets have little value if the company is liquidated. Therefore, a going-concern value should be determined. The price to be paid for this equipment should be somewhere within the range of the cost of new equipment or the cost of comparable used equipment. For this reason, an independent appraiser can be useful, particularly if he is acquainted with the type of equipment being sought or sold.

The seller should realize that he may own assets that do not appear on the fixed-asset schedule. Many companies have a policy of not capitalizing any assets below some arbitrary amount ($50 or $100). A complete physical inventory should be taken.

If the assets are numerous and geographically dispersed, the seller may be asked to prepare a certified list of the assets giving description and location. The buyer can then test the list by verifying only selected assets at the time of the sale, but with plans to verify all of them within a certain period of time.

The value of personal-property assets is usually decided after considerable bargaining. *It is better to assign values to individual assets rather than to make a lump-sum purchase of assets.* In a lump-sum purchase, there is more chance of overlooking some asset values.

The buyer should try to determine the condition of the assets as well as repair and replacement requirements. If he doesn't establish the condition of the assets individually, repair and possible replacement costs may create an unexpectedly heavy drain on his working capital.

Federal Income Tax Consequences

Federal income tax consequences of the buy-sell transaction may be an important bargaining issue if the buyer and seller are aware of them. The seller should be concerned about the amount of tax he will have to pay on his gains from the sale. The buyer should be concerned about the tax basis he will acquire as a result of the transaction. These concerns almost inevitably lead the buyer and seller into conflict in valuing the business.

The income-tax laws are highly technical, and the possible variations in a buy-sell situation are infinite. Because of this, a discussion specific enough to be really helpful is impossible here. Both buyer and seller should study the applicable sections of the IRS *Tax Guide for Small Business* [1]; and if an important decision in the buy-sell agreement is to be based on Federal income-tax consequences, the advice of an income-tax expert should be sought. The key to tax savings is tax planning—*before* the buy-sell contract is closed.

The seller should keep in mind that he must report any income-tax liability he incurs by selling a going business. Reinvesting the sales proceeds in another business will not enable him to avoid or postpone his income-tax liability.

A Valuation Example—the Regal Men's Store [2]

This example will help to bring the factors discussed about into better focus. It is not intended to show what *should* be done but to give some idea of what *might* be done.

The buyer and the seller. Joe Critser is interested in buying a men's clothing store. He has had nearly 25 years' experience in the men's clothing trade—first as a salesman in retail stores and more recently

---

[1] *Tax Guide for Small Business.* Revised annually and issued in December by the Internal Revenue Service. Superintendent of Documents, Washington, D.C. 20402.

[2] All names, dates, and places in this case are fictitious.

as a sales representative for Sentinel, a major manufacturer of men's clothing. Now 45 years old, Critser is interested in having a store of his own.

In February 1998 Critser learns that the Regal Men's Store is for sale. James Rombaugh, owner and operator of the store, is now 67 and wants to retire, he says. He has no heirs, and no employee of the store is financially able to purchase the business. Rombaugh started the store in the late twenties and has been the sole owner during the 40 years Regal has been in operation.

The store. Critser's early investigation convinces him that the store has the kind of possibilities he is looking for. Although it has been operated conservatively, it has a good reputation in the community and a creditable standing in the clothing trade. The store has never been particularly aggressive in advertising—the owner has relied on repeat patronage and word-of-mouth advertising.

Critser suspects that part of Rombaugh's desire to sell is due to competitive pressure from more aggressive stores in the community. Sales have continued to increase about in proportion to the market in general, but gross margin and profit have been reduced because of lower overall maintained markups and increasing costs of operation. Rombaugh owns the inventory, fixtures, equipment, and operating supplies and leases the building at 5 percent of net sales, with a minimum payment of $500 a month. The current lease will expire in about 4 years.

The preliminary discussion. Rombaugh has been well impressed with Critser and agrees to furnish necessary financial information. In their discussion to date, Rombaugh has stated that he feels the business is worth about $50,000 for the purchase of inventory, fixtures, equipment, and goodwill. He will retain all accounts receivable, but he is willing to allow the new owner an 8 percent fee for outstanding accounts receivable collected after the transfer of ownership has been completed.

He also wants to keep a few assets for which he has a sentimental attachment, such as a massive rolltop desk purchased when the store was first opened. Rombaugh will assume responsibility for payment of liabilities outstanding at the time of sale.

Critser, on the other hand, feels that the business is worth somewhat less than $50,000. It is obvious to him through casual inspection that some of the inventory is worth less than the original purchase price, and he doubts the value that Rombaugh would place on goodwill. He also notes that some of the display equipment is outmoded and needs replacement.

Before accepting or rejecting Rombaugh's price, Critser suggests that he be permitted to make his own evaluation of the business on the basis of past financial records and an appraisal of the assets. Rombaugh agrees. Following are the major elements of Critser's investigation and appraisal:

Past sales

1993—$110,000
1994— 114,400
1995— 119,000
1996— 123,800
1997— 128,800

Forecast sales—1998

$132,500—Critser's estimate of sales, which includes a somewhat smaller increase than the average of 4.3 percent per year between 1993 and 1997.

$134,338—Rombaugh's estimate based on the average.

Five-year operating statement

	1993	1994	1995	1996	1997
Sales....................	$110,000	$114,400	$119,000	$123,800	$128,800
Cost of goods sold.........	69,990	73,216	79,630	80,470	83,720
Gross margin...............	40,010	41,184	39,370	43,330	45,080
Operating expenses [1].......	31,210	33,176	31,337	35,283	37,352
Profit..............	$8,800	$8,008	$8,033	$8,047	$7,728

[1] Includes owner's salary of $7,000 per year.

Projected operating statement for 1998

	CRITSER (Buyer)	ROMBAUGH (Seller)
Sales................................	$132,500	$134,338
Cost of goods sold....................	86,125	87,320
Gross margin...................	46,375	47,018
Operating expenses [1]..................	38,425	37,883
Profit.......................	[2]$7,950	[3]$9,135

[1] Includes estimate of owner's salary.
[2] Based on 6 percent for 1998.
[3] Based on 6.8 percent, 5-year average.

Balance sheet of the Regal Men's Store as of January 31, 1998

Assets

Cash on hand and in bank..........................		$10,000
Accounts receivable......................	$16,000	
Less estimated uncollectible.............	2,000	
		14,000
Merchandise inventory..........................		24,607
Sales and office supplies.........................		960
Fixtures...............................	10,000	
Less estimated depreciation..............	2,800	
		7,200
Equipment.............................	9,500	
Less estimated depreciation..............	4,300	
		5,200
Miscellaneous assets..............................		640
Total assets................................		$62,607

Liabilities

Accounts payable.......................	$5,500	
Payroll and sales tax payable..............	650	
Total liabilities............................		$6,150

Net worth

James Rombaugh, capital.........................	56,457
Total liabilities and net worth...............	$62,607

Salable assets

Inventory at current book value....................	$24,607
Sales and office supplies............................	960
Fixtures, current depreciated value..................	7,200
Equipment, current depreciated value...............	5,200
Total salable assets.........................	$37,967

Valuation of inventory and appraisal of fixed assets

	CRITSER	ROM-BAUGH
Inventory by physical count........................		$23, 757
90 percent valued at current prices.......	$21, 381	
5 percent valued at 75 percent of current prices...........................	891	
5 percent valued at 50 percent of current prices...........................	594	
Inventory—appraised value...............	22, 866	23, 757
Usable office supplies....................	840	840
Fixtures—appraised value [1]................	6, 800	6, 800
Equipment—appraised value [1]............	4, 700	4, 700
Total assets—appraised value........	$35, 206	$36, 097

[1] Independent appraiser. Excludes assets to be retained by Rombaugh.

How much to pay? If Critser feels that his return on investment should be capitalized over 5 years, his offering price, based on anticipated profits for the year ahead, would be $39,750 (5 years=20 percent per year; $7,950÷.20=$39,750). If, on the other hand, the purchase was based on the appraised value of assets only, the purchase price would be $35,206 plus any provision for goodwill.

Since both of these figures are well below the suggested price of $50,000, negotiation will be necessary. Here are some questions that might arise:

1. In light of future sales and profit possibilities, are the assets worth more than the sale price?
2. Is the risk less than Critser anticipates? To pay $50,000, he would have to reduce his risk level to between 6 and 7 years.
3. Is Rombaugh's price too high in the light of future sales and profit possibilities under new management?
4. How much confidence does Critser have in his ability to realize an acceptable return on his investment?
5. Is the actual value of this business as a going concern closer to $34,000, $40,000, or $50,000?
6. How much is the goodwill of this business actually worth to Rombaugh? To Critser?
7. What kind of compromise might be satisfactory to both the buyer and the seller?

Chapter 7

Negotiating the Buy-Sell Contract

THE FINAL OBJECTIVE of the negotiation process is a written agreement covering the details of the proposed buy-sell transaction. Some of the details—price, terms of payment, price allocation, form of the transaction, liabilities, warranties—are matters over which the interests and motivations of the buyer and seller may be in sharp conflict.

The seller is interested in—

- The best possible price—
- Getting his money—
- Favorable tax treatment of gains from the sale—
- Severing liability ties, past and future—
- Avoiding contract terms and conditions that he may not be able to carry out.

In contrast, the buyer is interested in—

- A good title at the lowest possible price—
- Favorable payment terms—
- A favorable tax basis for resale and depreciation purposes—
- Warranty protection against false statements of the seller, inaccurate financial data, and undisclosed or potential liabilities—
- An indemnification agreement and security deposit.

The agreement reached by the parties, if they succeed in reaching one, will be the result of bargaining. Depending on the relative bargaining position of the buyer and seller, the buy-sell contract may reflect either compromise or capitulation.

Price

The central bargaining issue in the buy-sell transacton is price. Price is what is actually paid for a business. Value, as distinguished from price, relates to what the business is worth. The decisions of the buyer and seller as to how much to pay or take for each dollar of potential profit are a basis for bargaining, but other factors affect the final price.

In the Regal Men's Store negotiations, Rombaugh was asking $50,000 for his business. Critser made his own evaluation of the business and offered $33,000. After an extended period of negotiations, Critser and Rombaugh agreed on a purchase price of $42,000.

What determined the asking and offering prices? How did they finally arrive at the figure of $42,000?

The process of price determination is sometimes described as horse trading. This element is important, and undoubtedly both Rombaugh and Critser anticipated it in setting their asking and offering prices. But granting that tactics and compromise play a part in price determination, other explanations often account for the relative success or failure in the bargaining process.

Bargaining position. The price paid often reflects the bargaining position of one of the parties. Is the seller's desire to sell stronger than the buyer's desire to buy, or vice versa? The reason behind the decision to buy or sell is important. This would be true of a seller who must sell because of age, health, or personal financial reasons. If the buyer knows that sale of the business is urgent, the seller is less likely to get a reasonable price for his business, although the reasons bear no relation to the value of the business or the ability of the buyer to pay cash.

The seller's willingness to finance part of the price, or perhaps all of it, will also depend on the urgency of his need to sell. Sometimes a purchase price is agreed upon but later raised because the buyer is unable to get outside financing. The price may also be adjusted in order to get favorable tax treatment or in exchange for more favorable terms in other aspects of the contract.

The time factor. Another important factor affecting bargaining position is the time element—when to sell, when to buy. Economic conditions cannot be overlooked. The seller is more likely to gain his bargaining objectives when business conditions are good, particularly if his business is sharing the prosperity. During periods of recession— either general, local, or in a particular industry or activity—the pessimistic outlook of both buyers and sellers tends to depress prices.

The buyer. Still another important factor is, "Who is the buyer?" To a person experienced in business valuation, a business may be worth buying only at the liquidation value of the assets. To another buyer, the same business may be the answer to a long-held dream of owning his own business.

Liabilities

A buyer generally prefers to purchase assets rather than stock for tax reasons, but his preference becomes even stronger because of liability considerations. In the assets transaction, the legal continuity of the seller's business is broken. The seller's business liabilities are usually not carried over unless the buyer assumes them by agreement.

Buyers often find an advantage in assuming obligations of the seller under leases, mortgages, or installment-purchase contracts. The seller may be willing to make some financial sacrifice to the buyer in order to get out from under the payment burden—even though he remains liable for the obligation if the buyer defaults.

But these are known liabilities. It is the unknown that the buyer fears in the stock transaction. Many liabilities, both existing and potential, are unknown at the time of contracting merely because of inadequate investigation. And in any business, there are potential liabilities that neither an honest seller nor a diligent buyer can foresee at the time of the buy-sell transaction. An accident involving a company truck, the fall of a customer on the business premises, or the discharge of an employee may become the basis of a lawsuit and eventual liability, even though many months have passed since the event.

Even more elusive are liabilities that may arise from the manufacture or sale of defective products, patent or trademark infringements, or violations of statutes such as wage-and-hour laws, blue-sky laws, the Robinson-Patman Act, the Sherman Act, and so on. Tax deficiencies may arise out of tax returns filed but unaudited at the time of the buy-sell transaction.

The price agreed upon in a stock transaction will, of course, take into consideration only known liabilities. The possibility of unknown liabilities need not, however, preclude the buyer from entering into a stock transaction. Such a course of action may, in fact, be necessary in order to retain the benefits of nonassignable contracts, leases, franchises, government licenses, stock registrations, corporate name, and so on.

The buyer of stock should take precautions against unknown liabilities. Ordinarily this would include an agreement on the part of the seller to indemnify the buyer against such liabilities and on some means for satisfying any claims against the seller. Holding part of the purchase price in escrow against such a contingency gives the buyer at least some security.

Contract Terms

A number of problems in the buy-sell transaction are brought into focus by the necessity of "writing up a contract." At this point, agreement has usually been reached on the major issue—price. Presumably, the buyer and seller have considered tax consequences, assumption of liabilities, and terms of payment in arriving at a price.

More is involved in drafting an adequate buy-sell contract, however, than mechanically reducing these oral agreements to written form. To protect the interests of both parties, the contract must cover possible problems that are often far from the minds of the buyer and seller at the time.

What if the buyer defaults on his installment payment of the purchase price? What if the seller's financial statements, which the buyer relied on, turn out to be inaccurate or false? What if the seller turns out to have liabilities that have not been taken into account in the price? What if some of the assets purchased turn out not to be owned by the seller or are subject to undisclosed liens? What if material changes in the business occur before the buy-sell transaction is closed? What if the seller opens a competing business of the same type in the immediate vicinity?

These questions reflect the uncertainty of the buyer's position. The seller knows what he is selling and what he is getting (with a possible exception in the case of seller financing). The buyer is getting an unknown quantity. Whether or not the buyer gets the protection he should have as part of the contract is a matter of bargaining.

A Typical Buy-Sell Contract

Following is a typical buy-sell contract, with comments, covering the sale of the Regal Men's Store. The contract covers the sale of a proprietorship business, but the basic content would be the same in a corporate stock transaction.

———————•—•———————

THIS AGREEMENT is made and entered into this 15th day of February, 1998, between James Rombaugh, hereinafter referred to as the Seller, and Joe Critser, hereinafter referred to as the Buyer.

WHEREAS the Seller is the owner of a men's clothing store using the trade name of "Regal Men's Store" in Central City, Illinois, and the Seller desires to sell to the Buyer his rights, title and interests including the goodwill therein, and the Buyer is willing to buy the same on the terms and conditions hereinafter provided, IT IS AGREED AS FOLLOWS:

(The above statements introduce the parties and the nature of the agreement. If the business is incorporated and a stock transaction contemplated, the stockholders will be identified as the sellers and stock as the item sold.)

1. Sale of business. The Seller shall sell and the Buyer shall buy, free from all liabilities and encumbrances except as hereinafter provided, the men's clothing store owned and conducted by the Seller under the trade name of "Regal Men's Store" at the premises known as 120 North Main Street, Central City, Illinois, including the goodwill as a going concern, the lease to such premises, stock in trade, furniture, fixtures, equipment and supplies, all of which are more specifically enumerated in Schedule A attached hereto.

(Paragraph 1 incorporates by reference an inventory not shown here of the assets being purchased. A specific enumeration of assets being purchased is important as a basis for recourse against the seller in the event of shortage or title defects.)

2. Purchase price. The purchase price for all the assets referred to in paragraph 1 shall be $42,000 and allocable as follows:

Lease	0
Goodwill	$3, 000
Fixtures and equipment	15, 000
Inventory	23, 700
Supplies	300
	$42, 000

(The allocations in paragraph 2 represent compromise of the conflicting tax interests of the buyer and seller.)

3. Method of payment. The Buyer shall pay to the Seller the purchase price as stated above, in the following manner: (a) $5,000 by certified or cashier's check upon execution of this agreement, the receipt of which is hereby acknowledged by the Seller, such proceeds to be held in escrow by Paul Jones, attorney for the Seller, as provided in paragraph 13; (b) $20,000 by certified or cashier's check at the date of closing, subject to the adjustments provided for in paragraph 4; (c) the balance of $17,000 by a promissory note payable in consecutive monthly installments of $200 each beginning the first day of April, 1998, together with interest at 8% per annum. Such note shall contain a provision, satisfactory to the attorney for the Seller, for the acceleration of the balance remaining unpaid upon default in the payment of an installment for a period longer than thirty days. As security for the payment of any such note, the Buyer shall execute and deliver to the Seller at the closing a chattel mortgage upon the inventory, fixtures, and equipment described in paragraph 1, such mortgage to contain an after-acquired property clause and such other provisions as the attorney for the Seller may request.

(Paragraph 3 recognizes the financing seller's principal problem: security—or lack of it. The acuteness of the problem results from the fact that the buyer has usually exhausted all acceptable forms of security in getting the bank credit he needs.)

4. Adjustments. Adjustments shall be made at the time of closing for the following: inventory sold, insurance premiums, rent, deposits with utility companies, payroll and payroll taxes. The net amount of these adjustments shall be added or subtracted, as the case may be, from the amount due on the purchase price at the time of closing.

5. Buyer's assumption of contracts and liabilities. In the event this agreement to sell is in fact closed and the business is transferred by the Seller to the Buyer, the Buyer shall be bound by and does hereby assume the terms of the following contracts:

Lease of business premises dated January 1, 1996. The Buyer shall indemnify the Seller against any liability or expense arising out of any breach of such contracts occurring after the closing.

(Since a going business is being sold, the most realistic approach to the problem of outstanding liabilities may be for the buyer to assume all liabilities shown in an attached balance sheet and also liabilities that arise in the ordinary course of business after contracting but before closing. Such an agreement provides recourse by the seller against the buyer if the buyer defaults, but does not discharge the liability of the seller to the third party.)

6. Seller's warranties. The Seller warrants and represents the following:

(a) He is the owner of and has good and marketable title to all the assets specifically enumerated in Schedule A, free from all debts and encumbrances.

(b) The financial statements which are attached hereto as Schedule B have been prepared in conformity with generally accepted accounting principles and present a true and correct statement of the financial condition of said business as of their respective dates.

(c) There are no business liabilities or obligations of any nature, whether absolute, accrued, contingent or otherwise, except as and to the extent reflected in the balance sheet of January 31, 1998.

(d) No litigation, governmental proceeding or investigation is pending, or to the knowledge of the Seller threatened or in prospect, against or relating to said business.

(e) The Seller has no knowledge of any developments or threatened developments of a nature that would be materially adverse to said business.

(f) The statements made and information given by the Seller to the Buyer concerning said business, and upon which the Buyer has relied in agreeing to purchase said business, are true and accurate and no material fact has been withheld from the Buyer.

(Paragraph 6 is intended to protect the buyer from the unknown—title defects, undisclosed liens, false or fraudulent information, undisclosed or potential liabilities. If the buyer is becoming liable for all business liabilities through assumption or purchase of stock, he will require more extensive warranties than these.)

7. **Seller's obligation pending closing.** The Seller covenants and agrees with the Buyer as follows:

(a) The Seller shall conduct the business up to the date of closing in a regular and normal manner and shall use its best efforts to keep available to the Buyer the services of its present employees and to preserve the goodwill of the Seller's suppliers, customers and others having business relations with it.

(b) The Seller shall keep and maintain an accurate record of all items of inventory sold in the ordinary course of business from January 31, 1998 up until the date of closing. Such record shall be the basis for adjustment of the purchase price as provided in paragraph 4.

(c) The Seller shall give the Buyer or his representative full access during normal business hours to the business premises, records and properties, and shall furnish the Buyer with such information concerning operation of the business as the Buyer may reasonably request.

(d) The Seller shall comply to the satisfaction of the Buyer's attorney with all the provisions of the statute of the State of Illinois commonly known as the "Bulk Sales Act."

(e) The Seller shall deliver to the Buyer's attorney for examination and approval prior to closing such bills of sale and instruments of assignment as in the opinion of the Buyer's attorney shall be necessary to vest in the Buyer good and marketable title to the business, assets and goodwill of the Seller.

8. Risk of loss. The Seller assumes all risk of destruction, loss or damage due to fire or other casualty up to the date of closing. If any destruction, loss or damage occurs and is such that the business of the Seller is interrupted, curtailed or otherwise materially affected, the Buyer shall have the right to terminate this agreement. In such event, the escrow agent shall return to the Buyer the purchase money held by him. If any destruction, loss or damage occurs which does not interrupt, curtail or otherwise materially affect the business, the purchase price shall be adjusted at the closing to reflect such destruction, loss or damage.

(Paragraphs 7 and 8 are concerned with the period between contracting and actual transfer of ownership. The provisions stated anticipate such risks as depletion of inventory, injury to goodwill, creditors' actions, and casualty loss. In 7(c), the disruptive effect of a transfer of ownership is reduced by providing the buyer with the opportunity to become familiar with the details of the business operation before he assumes the responsibility of operation.)

9. Covenant not to compete. The Seller covenants to and with the Buyer, his successors and assigns, that for a period of five years from and after the closing he will not, directly or indirectly, either as principal, agent, manager, employee, owner, partner, stockholder, director or officer of a corporation, or otherwise, engage in any business similar to or in competition with the business hereby sold, within a fifty mile radius of Central City, Illinois.

(Paragraph 9 anticipates the possibility that the buyer would suffer a loss of the business goodwill he has purchased if the seller opened a similar business in competition with the buyer. Such provisions are enforceable if the restriction is reasonable. What is considered reasonable will depend on the circumstances of each case.)

10. Conditions precedent to closing. The Buyer's obligations at closing are subject to the fulfillment prior to or at closing of the following conditions:

(a) All of the Seller's representations and warranties contained in this agreement shall be true as of the time of closing.

(b) The Seller shall have complied with and performed all agreements and conditions required by this agreement to be performed or complied with prior to or at the closing.

(Paragraph 10 raises a problem that is inherent in the traditional contracting with a closing at some future date. In the period between, the buyer sometimes uncovers facts that would constitute a breach of warranty and grounds for canceling the contract. Because of this, transactions are finally closed, if at all, largely on the good faith of both parties. It is possible, if both parties work together toward the common goal, to sign the contract and close the transaction at the same time.)

11. Closing. The closing shall take place at the office of Paul Jones, 100 South Main Street, Central City, Illinois, on March 1, 1998, at 10:00 a.m. At the time of said closing, all keys to the business premises, the bills of sale and other instruments of transfer shall be delivered by the Seller to the Buyer and the money, note and mortgage required of the Buyer shall be delivered to the Seller. Upon completion of the said payment and transfer, the sale shall be effective and the Buyer shall take possession of the said business.

12. Indemnification by the seller. The Seller shall indemnify and hold the Buyer harmless against and will reimburse the Buyer on demand for any payment made by the Buyer after closing in respect to:

(a) Any liabilities and obligations of the Seller not expressly assumed by the Buyer.

(b) Any damage or deficiency resulting from misrepresentation, breach of warranty or nonfulfillment of the terms of this agreement.

13. Seller's security deposit. As security for the indemnities specified in paragraph 12, the Seller's attorney, Paul Jones, shall hold in escrow, for a period of one year from the date of closing, the sum of $5,000 which has been paid by the Buyer upon execution of this agreement. Said escrow agent shall upon application of the Buyer apply all or any part of such to reimburse the Buyer as provided in paragraph 12, provided the Seller shall have been given not less than ten days' notice of such application and has not questioned its propriety.

14. Arbitration of disputes. All controversies arising under or in connection with, or relating to any alleged breach of this agreement, shall be submitted to a panel of three arbitrators. Such panel shall be composed of two members chosen by the Seller and Buyer respectively and one member chosen by the arbitrators previously selected. The findings of such arbitrators shall be conclusive and binding on the parties hereto. Such arbitrators shall also conclusively designate the party or parties to bear the expense of such determination and the amount to be borne by each.

(Paragraph 12 obligates the seller to indemnify the buyer to the full extent of any cost or damage sustained by the buyer as a result of the seller's breach of warranty or contractual obligations. Paragraph 13 backs up this agreement with a requirement that part of the purchase price be placed in escrow as security for the seller's performance. Paragraph 14 provides a means for resolving without litigation any buyer-seller disputes that may arise from the contract.)

IN WITNESS WHEREOF, the Buyer and Seller have signed this agreement.

JAMES ROMBAUGH, *Seller*
JOE CRITSER, *Buyer*

Chapter 8

Financing and Implementing the Transaction

T HE BUYER AND SELLER have a number of important matters to attend to before the transaction can be closed. The seller will be thinking about instruments of transfer that must be delivered at the closing, about compliance with the bulk sale act, and possibly about making financial arrangements if the buyer can't raise the purchase price. The buyer's attention will be focused on financing arrangements, organizing his business-to-be, overseeing the seller's operation of the business in the meantime, and becoming familiar with the details of the business operation.

Compliance With the Bulk Sale Act

Most States require the seller of a business to furnish a sworn list of his creditors to the buyer and the buyer to give notice to the creditors of the pending sale. The purpose of such a "bulk sale" act is to make certain that the seller doesn't sell out his stock in trade and fixtures, pocket the proceeds, and disappear, leaving his creditors unpaid. Compliance with the statute gives creditors an opportunity to impound the proceeds of the sale if they think it necessary.

Noncompliance or inadequate compliance may result in attachment of the property after the sale by creditors of the seller and voiding of the buy-sell transaction. The buyer should not close the transaction until he has made sure that all statutory requirements have been met.

Financing the Buy-Sell Transaction

In general, the buyer has two options regarding the financing of the business. The first basic method of financing is personal investment of the future owner or owners of the business. The buyer may pay cash for the business out of personal resources, establish a partnership, or sell stock. These forms of financing are commonly referred to as the use of equity or investment capital.

The other basic form of financing is through borrowing or the establishment of credit. This method of financing may or may not require the payment of interest, but it does require the borrower to repay the principal, usually over a stipulated period of time or on a specific date. This method of financing is commonly referred to as the use of debt capital. Often the purchase is made through a combination of equity and debt capital.

Equity capital. In the simplest form of purchase, the buyer pays the full purchase price in cash. The buyer's investment in the business, at least initially, is full and complete. Whether the funds come from one person or more than one, the financial nature of the transaction does not change.

The sources of equity capital are many and varied. Generally, they are in the form of bank savings. Or cash may be obtained from liquidating certain assets the buyer may own, such as surrendering life insurance policies for cash value or selling real estate, stocks and bonds, or other assets.

Before disposing of assets, however, the buyer should ask himself this question: "Do I want to buy the business more than I want to keep these assets, considering both present and future values?" For instance, if the buyer cashes $8,000 worth of government bonds, there may be a possibility of his making a higher profit, but the risk of losing his investment entirely will be greater. He should be as certain as possible that the expected return is worth the risk.

An equally important question is how much the buyer should invest in the business. In general, the more he invests himself, the better chance he will have of borrowing at least part of the purchase price.

A buyer may not have the capital, however, nor perhaps the inclination, to purchase the business outright with his own personal funds. How far he goes in this respect depends on his own cash resources, his confidence in the business, and his ability to borrow money or establish credit with others.

Debt capital. In most cases, the buyer of a small business will have to borrow money or establish credit to purchase the business. Several factors will affect the use of debt capital for this purpose: the source of capital, the amount that can be borrowed, and the length of time for which the capital can be borrowed.

Commercial lending institutions are the sources to which the buyer will probably turn first. The availability of financing through these sources depends on the security that can be pledged to the loan, the profit potential of the business, the prospect of repayment of principal and interest, and the general availability of credit.

One of the major difficulties facing the buyer at this point concerns the collateral that can be pledged as security. The physical assets of the business—particularly fixtures, equipment, and land and buildings—will not be available for security unless they are free of other financial obligations. The buyer may be forced to look to his own personal assets, such as cash value of life insurance, stocks and bonds, mortgages on real property, and so on.

Less formal sources of debt capital may be open to the buyer, such as loans from friends, relatives, business associates, and the like. Many small businesses have been financed through such means.

The seller as lender. A common source of debt capital is that supplied by the seller when he lets the buyer pay for the business over time. Why should the seller finance the buyer? Probably because the desire to sell is strong enough so that the seller is willing to assume part of the risk.

As in financing from other sources, the seller usually demands that the buyer pay interest on the amount being financed and repay the principal and interest at stipulated periods. The seller usually establishes his security on the more certain assets, such as fixtures and equipment. However, he may also assume the inventory as acceptable security without placing it in a bonded warehouse.

The seller's philosophy toward financing the buyer seems to be that if the buyer should fail, the seller can take back the business. The major problem in this form of financing is that it is harder for the buyer to get additional financing from other sources when the seller has first claim on the assets of the business.

How much to borrow. As the first step toward financing the purchase of a business, the buyer has to find answers to two questions:

"How much do I need to borrow?"

"How much can I afford to borrow?"

The answer to the first question depends partly on how much money the buyer has and how much he is willing to invest in the business himself. The less equity capital he has, the more debt capital he needs.

How much he can afford to borrow depends on his ability to keep up principal and interest payments. If a buyer borrows from a number of sources, he may find himself committed to a repayment schedule that the profits from the business will not support. His borrowing plans should be related to the projected income statement prepared during his study of the business under consideration.

Operating capital. In addition to funds for purchasing the business, the buyer must have enough working capital to cover the cost of operation until the business itself produces enough cash. In other words, the buyer must think in terms of cash requirements and cash flow for weeks and months ahead. A common mistake in buying a business is failure to provide adequate working capital.

If sales and business costs after purchase of the business are expected to follow the pattern of the immediate past, the need for short term working capital should not be hard to estimate.

Closing the Sale of the Regal Men's Store

In the sale and purchase of the Regal Men's Store, discussed in chapters 6 and 7, Rombaugh and Critser compromised on a price of $42,000. The problem then facing the two men was how the transaction was to be financed. What were the various possibilities?

• *Critser could pay the entire $42,000 out of cash or negotiable assets converted to cash, providing he had that amount and was willing to invest the entire sum.* Critser did not have that much cash and was not likely to be able to raise it.

• *Critser could pay up to the limit of his own resources and borrow the rest.* Critser had been turned down by three banks—they did not consider him an acceptable credit risk. This had nothing to do with Critser's personal credit rating. It was due to concern about whether he could meet the resulting financial obligations out of profits and about the nature of the assets as a basis for security.

• *Rombaugh could allow Critser to assume ownership of the business and pay the amount due over several years.* Whether Rombaugh would agree to such an arrangement would depend on how badly he wanted to sell to Critser, how long it would take Critser to pay off the amount due, and whether there were any other potential buyers who might be able to finance the purchase differently.

• *Critser might be able to get others to invest with him, forming a partnership and spreading the capital requirements among two or more owners.* This arrangement would reduce Critser's ownership in the business, since the legal form would be changed from a single proprietorship to a partnership. Critser did not want this. He would rather not purchase the business than take on a partner.

• *Critser might form a corporation and sell stock to raise capital.* This would not ordinarily be feasible for such a small business. The cost of complying with stock registration requirements, the possibility of losing control of management, the lack of a market for such securities, and the greater relative cost of equity capital over debt capital would all work against it.

Plan for Financing the Purchase

Critser's personal investment.................. p......		$20, 000
Financed by Rombaugh...........................		17, 000
First-year payment:		
Principal at $200 a month......	$2, 400	
Interest at 8 percent..........	1, 360	
	$3, 760	
Financed by Hirschberger.................		5, 000
First-year payment:		
Principal....................	$1, 667	
Interest at 8 percent..........	400	
	2, 067	
First-year principal and interest payments....	$5, 827	
Total price...............................		$42, 000

Regal Men's Store

Balance Sheet, February 15, 1998

Assets

Cash on hand and in bank............................	$2, 000
Merchandise inventory...............................	23, 700
Fixtures and equipment..............................	15, 000
Sales and office supplies............................	300
Goodwill...	3, 000
Total assets..................................	$44, 000

Liabilities

Notes payable.......................................	$22, 000

Net Worth

Joe Critser, capital................................	22, 000
Total liabilities and net worth..................	$44, 000

The decision. In effect, the only course of financing open to Critser was to raise as much as possible, borrow from personal sources, and enlist Rombaugh's willingness to finance the balance. Rombaugh agreed to finance the business to the extent of $17,000, accepting a chattel mortgage on inventory, fixtures, and equipment.

This is somewhat unusual, particularly as to the inventory. There was no requirement that the inventory be placed in a bonded warehouse or otherwise controlled. Rombaugh based his decision on his own knowledge of average inventory value and on his willingness to accept the risk that Critser would not tie up further purchases in accounts payable.

With Rombaugh financing $17,000, Critser now had to raise the remaining $25,000. He got $5,000 in the form of a loan from his former boss Dan Hirschberger. As security, Critser pledged some stock he owned. He agreed to repay the loan semiannually over a 3-year period at 8 percent interest.

The cash value of Critser's life insurance and his Series E Bonds brought $8,000 and $7,000 respectively. Another $5,000 came from his wife—savings she had accumulated working as a secretary. A $2,000 inheritance Critser had received several years before was to be retained for use as working capital, and this would be supplemented by the 8 percent fee he would receive from Rombaugh for collecting the accounts receivable outstanding at the time of purchase. This fee would amount to about $1,100 if all the accounts were collected.

How it all stacks up. With these arrangements, Critser's financial position with regard to the purchase of the business was as shown in the box on page 62. Almost everything he owned was either invested in or pledged to the business. One question remained: Would the business bring in enough cash to cover operating costs and other financial obligations?

The outcome—what will it be? Should he have bought the business? Can he meet his financial obligations? Will he be able to maintain enough working capital to replace inventory, pay his operating costs, and repay his debt capital with interest as the payments fall due?

Only time will tell how good a manager Critser is. Many businesses have been bought and operated successfully on a more precarious start than this. Perhaps he will prove capable of meeting the challenge. Perhaps not.

If he should fail what would he lose? Practically everything—his full investment of $20,000 plus whatever else is necessary beyond the sale value of the assets to satisfy his creditors. Whether he succeeds or fails will depend on how well he can administer the financial program of the store, how well he can merchandise, how well he can keep his costs in line, how near his sales come to his earlier estimates.

Part 4

Using Financial Statements
in the Buy-Sell Transaction

Chapter 9

Income Statements
and Balance Sheets

THE DISCUSSION OF FINANCIAL STATEMENTS in this chapter assumes that the statements are prepared in accordance with generally accepted accounting principles. Here is a brief statement of some of the more important of these principles:

• A business should have financial reports prepared at the end of each calendar or fiscal year, with interim reports during the year. Use of the "natural" business year as the formal accounting period has been increasing. The natural year is the 12-month period ending at the lowest point of business activity for the period.

• Since many business transactions will be incomplete at the end of any accounting period, some estimates will be necessary. Such estimates are an acceptable part of financial reports as long as they are made according to procedures that have proved reliable in the past.

• Each business is considered a separate accounting unit, with the affairs of the business kept entirely separate from the owner's personal affairs. All records and reports should be prepared on this basis.

• Financial statements are prepared on the assumption that the business unit will continue to function in its usual manner.

• For some accounting objectives, two or more methods are possible. For example, there are several methods of computing depreciation and also of valuing inventory. They are all valid, but once a method has been selected for use in the records of a business, it should be used consistently.

- Accounting must be practical. Strict adherence to a principle is not required when the increase in accuracy is too small to justify the increased cost of compliance. A uniform policy should be adopted to guide such exceptions, however.

- All assets and services required by a business should be recorded on the date they are acquired at their cost to the business. This cost includes costs incurred to procure the asset or service and to place it in position or condition for business use. Donated assets are recorded at their cash equivalent value as of the date of donation.

- A major objective of accounting is to determine income by matching costs against revenue. The net income of a business is the increase in that company's net assets brought about through profitable exchanges of product and services or through sale of assets other than stock in trade.

What Is Being Sold

In the usual buy-sell transaction relating to a "going concern," what is being bought or sold is primarily a future stream of income. Not the assets or property of the business, but the income these assets will generate in the future. But future income is impossible to compute and hard to estimate. Therefore, the buyer and seller often ignore this unknown quantity. In trying to set the price, they concern themselves with known values relating principally to the replacement cost of the tangible assets being sold. This is a mistake.

Use of Past Financial Data in Valuing Future Income

It has been said that history repeats itself, but this is not always true of the financial history of a business. First of all, the question arises, "Why is the present owner willing to sell the business?" One reason may be that he foresees adverse change of one sort or another.

Keep in mind, too, in trying to predict the future from present results, that there will be a change of ownership. Will the new owner be able to produce the results the former owner did? Is he trained and experienced in management as well as in the mechanical or technical skills needed?

There are many reasons why past operating results may not be a good indication of future income. Still, they are at least concrete facts. They should be examined carefully for whatever insight they may provide into the future.

What Data To Expect

Most businesses will have at least two basic financial statements prepared at the end of the annual accounting period—a statement of income and a balance sheet. There may also be other statements containing important information. These might include a reconciliation of retained earnings in the business, a statement of source and application of funds, and listings of such items as inventories, accounts receivable, and accounts payable. However, the statement of income and the balance sheet are the basic financial statements. Any business can reasonably be expected to have these two available.

If they have not been prepared, it may be necessary to construct approximate statements—particularly statements of income—based on the best information available. If they are available but were not prepared in accordance with generally accepted accounting principles, they will probably have to be adjusted.

It is essential to understand what the accountant means by the amounts shown on the financial statements. The items discussed below should appear on most such statements. The listing is not all-inclusive, but most major items are discussed.

The Balance Sheet

A balance sheet lists in one section all the assets of the business as of the last day of the accounting period and in another section all claims against these assets. Claims against assets include creditors' claims, or liabilities, and owner's claims, or investment (also called equity or net worth).

Assets

Cash. This asset includes cash balances in the bank, cash on hand (including change and petty-cash funds), funds held in trust, sinking funds, and funds in time deposits. Not all the cash will necessarily be available for payment of liabilities. Change funds, for example, must be retained in order to have the change necessary for doing business.

Marketable securities. Included in this classification are such items as United States Treasury bills and perhaps stocks and bonds. These assets are most commonly shown on the balance sheet at their cost to the business or at their market value.

Accounts receivable. An entry that is identified merely as "accounts receivable" or has the designation "trade" after it refers to accounts receivable from customers only. Notes or accounts receivable from officers, employees, or owners of the business are considered nontrade receivables and should be entered as a separate item.

Allowance for bad debts. This is an account that is deducted from the accounts-receivable account to give a more accurate valuation to accounts receivable. Suppose the business has accounts receivable of $50,000 and experience indicates that 5 percent of this amount will be uncollectible. There is no way of knowing which specific accounts will not be collected, but it can be estimated that $2,500 will eventually be uncollectible. To reflect this fact on the balance sheet, accounts receivable are shown at $50,000. An allowance for bad debts of $2,500 is also entered and deducted from the accounts receivable, leaving a net of $47,500 as the estimated collectible accounts receivable.

Notes receivable. This account includes the face amount of all notes that have been given the company and that are still unmatured, even those that have been discounted at the bank.

Notes receivable discounted. This is a contingent (possible) liability account. If a note receivable has been discounted at the bank, the company has had to guarantee its payment. Thus, until the maker of the note pays the bank, the company has a possible note payable.

The amount of the notes receivable discounted is entered on the balance sheet under the notes receivable entry and subtracted from the notes receivable total. An alternative method is not to include it in the notes receivable total but to show it in a footnote.

Notes and accounts receivable from officers, employees, and owners. This amount will include amounts due the business from persons connected with the business in some way. Advances for employees' uniforms or cash loans may have been made, for instance.

Inventories. Inventories are the major asset in some kinds of businesses, particularly those in the merchandising field. Methods of valuing inventories are similar in manufacturing and nonmanufacturing companies, but the mechanics of computing the values differ. Therefore, valuation methods are discussed separately.

Purchased inventories. If the business buys merchandise or raw materials which it merely holds for a time and then sells with little or no alteration, the inventory is valued either at cost or at the replacement price if the latter is below cost. If the replacement price is higher than cost, the inventory should be valued at cost.

It is generally agreed that if the cost of transportation of the goods to the company is a significant item, the inventory account should include this cost. In fact, all costs involved in preparing the goods for sale could justifiably be included. Such costs might include, for example, certain costs of dividing and repackaging.

Once it has been decided what costs are to be included in the inventory account, there are at least four major methods of valuing the inventory:

1. If a business specifically identifies items in costing inventory, it must be able to tell what was paid for each item. This method is practical for items with a high unit price, such as new automobiles or major appliances. As the unit price falls, however, and the number of items in the inventory increases, this method of valuation becomes less practical.

2. First in, first out, or FIFO, is another method of costing inventory. It assumes that the first units purchased are the first units sold, that those still in inventory are the last ones purchased. Thus, the inventory is valued at the cost price of the last items purchased by the business.

3. Last in, first out, or LIFO, assumes the opposite—that the last goods purchased are the first ones sold. The inventory is thus valued at the cost of the first inventory items to be available for selling. The inventory valuation under LIFO does not necessarily correspond very closely to current replacement costs.

4. The average cost method is merely an average of FIFO and LIFO. It aims to find a middle ground between the two extremes.

If prices of the goods purchased have been rising, the FIFO valuation will come closest to current market prices—the use of LIFO will tend to value the inventory at less than current market prices. The choice of inventory valuation will affect the reported cost of goods sold on the income statement and also the reported net income.

Manufactured inventories. If the company manufactures goods from purchased raw materials, the inventory costing or valuation method is somewhat different. Any raw materials on hand are valued by one of the methods described for purchased inventories. Valuation of work in process and finished goods inventories involves three elements:

1. *Cost of the raw materials used.* This can be computed very exactly.

2. *Cost of the direct labor used in converting the raw material into its present state of completion.* This, too, normally lends itself to fairly exact measurement.

3. *Factory overhead, or indirect cost.* These are the costs of such items as insurance, indirect materials, indirect labor, taxes, and so on. They must be allocated to the units produced on some reasonable basis.

Total indirect costs do not vary with the amount of goods produced, or at least not proportionately. This means that if the plant is not operated at its maximum capacity, the indirect costs per unit of production will be more than would be the case if the plant were operated at a higher level of production. Therefore, idle time or idle capacity in a plant may cause the inventory value of manufactured goods to be unrealistically high.

Prepaid and deferred items. Prepaid expenses are prepayments for goods or services that will be consumed in the near future—prepaid rent, prepaid insurance premiums, office supplies, and so on. Deferred charges are prepayments that will benefit the company over a period of years, such as the cost of moving to a new location.

Property, plant, and equipment. This classification includes all the fixed assets of the business—land, buildings, equipment, and other tangible items that will last more than a year and will be used in the normal operation of the business. These items, under generally accepted accounting principles, should be recorded at their original cost to the business.

Occasionally, a buyer may find that the seller has raised the valuation of these assets by appraisal writeups. If this has occurred, the buyer must satisfy himself that the value of the assets has in fact increased by the amount of the appraisal writeup.

Accumulated depreciation and depletion. This account shows the amount of depreciation, or loss of usefulness, that has been charged against the property, plant, and equipment while they have been held by the business. On the balance sheet, the amount in each depreciation account is deducted from the corresponding property, plant or equipment total. This leaves the net book value, or unrecovered original cost.

A depreciation account is merely a technique for distributing the cost of a fixed asset over its *estimated* useful life. It is quite possible for assets that are fully depreciated on the books to be still serviceable, and for assets not fully depreciated to be no longer serviceable.

There are a number of methods of figuring depreciation. Four of the most common are the straight-line method, the declining-balance method, the sum-of-the-years-digits method, and the units-of-production method.

The first three methods record depreciation on the basis of time. The straight-line method records the depreciation uniformly over the years of the asset's estimated service life. It is by far the most commonly used because of its simplicity. The declining-balance and sum-of-the-years-digits methods record larger amounts of depreciation in the early years. With these two methods, increased maintenance expenses in later years are offset somewhat by the reduced charges for depreciation. Also, there are some income-tax advantages.

The units-of-production method is based on the estimated productive capacity of the asset rather than time. It is useful where the amount of usage varies considerably from time to time.

All four methods will record the same total depreciation over the life of the asset. There may be a substantial difference in the amount recorded in any one year, however.

Intangibles. This classification includes such items as patents, trademarks, and goodwill. The value recorded is their cost to the business. The amount entered for a patent, for example, will be either the cost of purchasing the patent right or the cost of developing the patent. Goodwill will not appear on the balance sheet unless the business purchased the goodwill and has decided to leave it on the books.

Liabilities and Owner's Equity

Accounts payable to trade. The amounts recorded in this account are the amounts owed to regular trade creditors (except notes payable) for merchandise and other items needed in operating the business.

Notes payable. This item includes all amounts owed by the business for which a formal note payable has been given if the note is due in 12 months or less from the balance-sheet date.

Accrued taxes payable. This account will show the amounts owed to various taxing authorities. It will include taxes that have been collected or withheld but not yet forwarded to the authorities—for example, sales taxes, income withholding taxes, and Federal Insurance Contribution Act (Social Security) taxes. The account may also include accruals for items such as property taxes, franchise taxes, and use taxes the business owes but has not yet been paid. The amount shown on the balance sheet should be the amount that the business is legally liable for.

Wages and salaries payable. This account will show all wages and salaries of employees earned but not paid as of the balance-sheet date. Any unclaimed wages due former employees will also be included in this account.

There are some rather rigid legal requirements about the handling of taxes collected from the employees as opposed to ordinary business liabilities.

Income taxes payable. This account may not appear on the balance sheet if the business is operated as a single proprietorship or partnership. It should be shown for a corporation. The amount may be only an estimate but will usually be quite accurate.

Unearned income. Some types of businesses receive fairly large amounts of prepaid or unearned income. The publisher of a newspaper or periodical, for instance, is paid for subscriptions before the publications are delivered. If a business rents property to others, the rent will be received in advance. The amount of such income that has been received but not earned at the balance-sheet date is recorded here. There may or may not be a legal requirement that the unearned amounts be returned if the company fails to deliver the services or products.

Long-term liabilities. For a liability to be considered long term, its maturity date should be more than 12 months from the balance-sheet date. If unearned income is prepayment for services covering more than a year from the balance-sheet date, a proportionate amount of it should be included here instead of under unearned income.

Owner's equity. Two elements enter into owner's equity: the initial investment of the owner or owners, and retained profit or loss. The computation of owner's equity is based on the recorded value of the assets and liabilities of the business—it is merely the difference between the total assets and the total liabilities. If the assets are recorded at less than their true value, the owner's equity will be understated. If the assets are recorded at an inflated value, the owner's equity will be overstated.

If the business is a corporation, the original investments of the owners will be kept in separate contributed capital accounts. The net results of operations will be summarized in one or more retained earnings accounts. All these accounts together make up the owners' investment in the business.

If the business is a single proprietorship or a partnership, each owner will have a capital account that summarizes his investments, his share of net income or losses, and withdrawals he has made.

Income Statement

The income statement is a summary of the income and expenses of the business for the period covered. It shows the net result of operations— profit or loss—for the period.

Revenue. All income of the business from whatever source should be included. However, income from operations is usually shown separately from other income such as interest or rent. Charge sales are included in sales income at the time the sale is made, regardless of when the cash is received in payment.

74

Cost of goods sold. The cost of goods sold equals the cost of goods purchased during the accounting period (including transportation) plus the beginning inventory and minus the ending inventory.

Gross margin. This is the difference between income from operations and cost of goods sold. The gross margin must cover operating expenses, taxes, and profit.

Operating expenses. Types of operating expenses vary with the type of business, but all businesses have some—building expenses, utilities, wages, supplies, some kinds of taxes, insurance, and so on. These expenses for the accounting period are subtracted from the gross margin to give the net income (before income taxes).

Auditing of Financial Statements

If the buyer in a buy-sell transaction asks an accountant to audit the financial statements of the seller, the accountant will want to make a "purchase investigation." A purchase investigation is a normal audit with intensified examination of certain items critical in a buy-sell situation. The accountant may go to greater lengths, for example, to make sure that the physical plant and all equipment are present and in serviceable condition.

There is no required form an accountant must use in certifying financial statements, but the following standard certificate has evolved:

> We have examined the balance sheet of the_____ Company as of December 31, ____ and the related statement of income and surplus for the year then ended. Our examination was made in accordance with generally accepted auditing standards and accordingly included such tests of the accounting records and such other auditing procedures as we considered necessary in the circumstances.
>
> In our opinion the accompanying balance sheet and statement of income and surplus present fairly the financial position of the_____Company at December 31, ____ and the results of its operations for the year then ended, in conformity with generally accepted accounting principles applied on a basis consistent with that of the preceding year.

If the accountant cannot use this certificate as it is, he will do one of two things. He will either qualify his certification, or state that he is unable to render an opinion regarding the financial statements. This might happen if he were unable to comply with generally accepted auditing standards, or if the accounting records were not prepared in conformity with generally accepted accounting principles.

What If There Are No Financial Statements?

The buyer may find, in a very small business, that the owner has never prepared financial statements. Furthermore, there may be no records available from which to prepare them.

There is no realistic way to determine the results of past operations without financial statements. However, there are a few records that even the smallest, most poorly run business must have. The buyer should try to construct from these records as realistic as possible an income statement and balance sheet. Here are some of these records:

• The seller will have had to file Federal income-tax returns that include an income statement for the business. At least part of this income statement will probably have been prepared on a cash basis and will not reflect the results of operations as accurately as a statement prepared on an accrual basis would. However, it is a fairly safe bet that the seller has not overstated the receipts from the business on his income-tax return. He may have tended to overstate expenses, though, particularly by including some personal expenses as expenses of the business.

• If the seller has a retail store and make sales in a State that has a sales tax, he has had to file sales-tax returns. The buyer should examine these returns to determine the amount of gross sales during the period covered.

• If the business has employees, the seller will have made deductions from the employees' pay for income taxes and Social Security. The returns prepared for the Director of Internal Revenue covering these deductions will show the wages paid.

• Almost any business will have certain types of expenses such as property taxes and insurance. The buyer can call the County Treasurer and the insurance agent to learn the amounts of these expenses.

• A fairly good evaluation of the financial position of the business can be made by talking to the seller's principal suppliers and to his bank to determine the amounts owed by the seller and the credit standing of the business.

Adjustments to the Financial Statements

IT IS IMPORTANT TO KNOW what the accountant who audits and certifies the financial statements is saying. He is *not* saying that there is no possibility of error in the financial statements. He *is* saying that the financial statements substantially reflect the correct financial position of the business. His certificate on a set of financial statements is the buyer's assurance that he can rely on the statements without further investigation to determine that they were prepared correctly. Some adjustments may be needed, however, to make the statements more useful in valuing the business.

Assets

Cash. No revaluation of this item is likely to be needed unless the business has deposits in foreign currencies. In that case, a revaluation may be necessary for possible loss in conversion of foreign currencies into United States dollars.

The buyer should also be aware that some of the cash may not be available to pay current debt and operating expenses. For example, some cash may have to be kept in change and petty-cash funds.

Marketable securities. Marketable securities are often recorded on the balance sheet at their cost, which may be below current market value. These assets should be stated at market value. Short-term

Treasury notes or bonds that will mature shortly after the sale of the business could be valued at their maturity value. There would probably be little difference between this and their market value.

Accounts receivable and allowance for bad debts. These two accounts must be examined together. The buyer should make certain that the net receivables on the balance sheet are really collectible.

The most common way to do this is to prepare an aging of the accounts receivable to show how old each account is. Thus, if the business normally sells merchandise on 30 days' credit and many of their accounts receivable are more than 90 days old, it is doubtful that these accounts can be collected.

If there are large accounts due from individual customers, the buyer might be wise to correspond directly with the customers to verify the amounts receivable. At the very least, invoices and signed shipping receipts should be studied to make sure that the customers have received the merchandise and have not yet paid for it.

The objective of the valuation of the accounts receivable is to state them at the true net collectible amount.

Notes receivable and notes receivable discounted. These two accounts must also be examined together. Unless the business normally receives a note at the time of a sale, a note from a customer usually means that the customer was unable to pay his account when it was due. The customer has, therefore, already shown some financial weakness, and the number of notes that will prove uncollectible may be fairly high. The buyer should try to find out whether notes still held by the business are likely to be paid at maturity.

The objective is to state the notes at their estimated collectible value and the amounts the business is likely to have to pay on default of discounted notes.

Accounts receivable and notes receivable from officers, employees, and owners. Since these items represent amounts due from people who have an inside interest in the business, there may be a serious question as to whether they will be collectible. Care should be taken to see that they are stated at their realizable value to the business.

Inventories. If inventories are stated on the balance sheet at cost, this cost may be what was paid recently, or it may be only indirectly related to the present value of the inventory. If the buyer does not feel competent to appraise the condition of the inventory, he should obtain the services of someone who is. He should not rely on the valuation of the seller.

One way to verify or correct the inventory value in a small business is to get the company's supplier to value the inventory. This is especially suitable if one principal vendor supplies the business. Since he or his representative will have to visit the business regularly in the future, it will be to his advantage to make sure that the valuation is fair. Also, the suppliers know the value of their own goods. The valuation should allow for all trade discounts and damaged or obsolete stock should be rejected.

Prepaid and deferred items. These items will be valued at their unrecovered cost to the business. The buyer should make sure that he can use any prepaid items he buys. Suppose, for example, that the business has recently purchased substantial quantities of stationery and other printed office supplies bearing the name of the present owner. Unless the name of the business is to be carried over, any amount that appears in the prepaid items for these supplies should be removed.

The buyer should also make sure that any prepaid insurance premiums and the insurance policies to which they apply can be transferred to him without loss of coverage or requirement for additional premium payments. He should be aware that premiums on workmen's compensation insurance are subject to later adjustment. Any insurance the buyer doesn't want, of course, will be canceled, and the balance sheet should be adjusted to show this.

Property, plant, and equipment. A professional appraisal of buildings, plant, and equipment may be useful, but many intangibles enter into a selling price. The fact that the building is appraised at $50,000 doesn't necessarily mean that the building is worth that much to the buyer. On the other hand, it may be worth more.

Another common way to value an asset of this kind is to establish a replacement value, allow depreciation for the length of time the asset has been held, and use the remainder as the value of the asset. The main problem in using replacement value is that fixed assets are seldom replaced with identical assets. A 20-year-old building is not likely to be replaced with a building just like it. Building methods change and needs of the business change. Therefore, it is unrealistic to think in terms of replacement cost for an asset that would never be replaced.

The seller of the business may want to value these fixed assets on the basis of values established by the insurance company in determining the amount of fire and extended-coverage insurance. The buyer should realize that these values are not necessarily equal to sale or market values. There is probably no one good way to value assets of this kind. Their true value will depend on the amount of income that can be generated through their use.

Intangibles. Intangible assets are recorded on the balance sheet at their cost to the business less any amounts written off. The buyer is mainly concerned with whether the intangibles really exist and will benefit the business in the future. Patents and trademarks may have a market value and could, in some cases, be sold. But their market value is very hard to determine until they are sold.

The buyer may recognize that patents and trademarks will benefit the business but be unable to determine the degree of usefulness with any accuracy. He should at least recognize that patents have a limited life, and he should find out how much time is left before the patent expires. A trademark, if registered, is not limited and may benefit the business indefinitely.

Any goodwill on the balance sheet reflects an amount paid at some time in the past, less what has been charged off. There is no assurance that any goodwill still attaches to the business.

In the case of liquidation, intangibles are usually of no value. Anything paid for them is not likely to be recoverable.

Claims Against Assets

Accounts payable to trade. If the business is in financial difficulties, the creditors may be willing to adjust downward the amounts due them. In that case, the balance-sheet item should be adjusted to show only the amount required to satisfy the creditors' adjusted claims.

If some of the accounts are past due, it may be found that some of the creditors have mechanics' liens against assets of the business. This is primarily a legal matter. The buyer should consult his lawyer about this possibility.

Notes payable. It is possible that substantial interest accrued on notes payable has not been entered in the accounts of the business. This account should be valued at the face amount of the notes plus interest accrued up to the date of the buy-sell agreement. If some of the notes are past their maturity dates, the buyer should consult his lawyer about the possibility of pending legal action against the business.

Accrued taxes payable. These amounts due are subject to audit by the taxing authority concerned. It is entirely possible that past discrepancies or failure to report taxes due might result in substantial penalties, interest, and back tax payments.

The buyer should try to ensure that a clear distinction is made between the seller's responsibility for taxes collected in the past and the buyer's responsibility for future tax liabilities. He must make certain that the account properly reflects all sales taxes collected and not yet remitted to the taxing authorities; all withholding and FICA taxes collected and not yet remitted; all unemployment taxes; all franchise taxes; and all excise taxes. He should also make certain that the business is not liable for any taxes it has failed to collect in the past.

Federal and State income taxes payable. A business organized as a single proprietorship or partnership does not pay income taxes as a business and therefore will not have this account. If the business is a corporation, the buyer should see that Federal and State income taxes of the business have been paid and that there is an adequate income tax accrual in the books for current income taxes payable. If income taxes have been improperly reported in past years, the corporation, even if it has changed hands, will have to pay any back taxes, penalties, and interest assessed against it.

Unearned revenues. The principal concern here is to make certain that all unearned revenues that have been collected are included in this account. Some businesses may record unearned revenues as earned revenues at the time of receipt.

Long-term liabilities. Most long-term liabilities will be evidenced by a formal agreement such as a note payable or a mortgage payable. They should be valued at the total amount owed, including interest.

Unrecorded liabilities. It is always possible that some notes payable, accounts payable, or accrued liabilities have not been included in the sellers' latest balance sheet. The buyer should be aware of this possibility and make at least a reasonable search for unrecorded liabilities such as these.

Contingent liabilities. This broad group includes a number of items that *may* become liabilities to the business even after it changes hands. Usually few, if any, contingent liabilities appear on the seller's balance sheet.

For example, a delivery truck owned by the business may have been involved in a serious accident. If the business had inadequate insurance protection, there is a very real possibility that the business will have to pay substantial claims. Or perhaps warranties, express or implied, go with the merchandise or services sold. Future costs may be involved in honoring warranties already given by the seller. Such items could conceivably have an appreciable impact on the future profitability of the business.

The searching out of contingent liabilities is difficult. In fact, there may be no way to discover some of them. But any prospective buyer should search out whatever information he can about contingent liabilities of the business he is considering. Some of these investigations might best be done by the buyer's attorney. If the buyer knows the real answer to the question "Why is the seller willing to sell?" he may decide the business is not a good investment.

Owner's equity. If the above examination of the balance sheet has resulted in any changes in assets or liabilities, the owner's equity will have to be adjusted. It must equal the difference between total assets and total liabilities.

Income Statement

The buyer should examine the income statement closely to make certain that it gives a reasonably accurate picture of the results of past operations. He should determine that the revenues reported on the income statement were earned in the period covered by the statement. No prepaid or unearned revenues should be included in the income reported, and no revenue items that properly apply to the period should be omitted.

Expenses. Expenses should be examined to determine that all have been included and that all items included are proper expenses of the business. If any personal living expenses of the owners have been paid by the business and included as business expense, these items should be eliminated.

Owner's salary. The amount of salary paid the owner is always a troublesome area. It may appear too high—or completely inadequate. The buyer should know the market value of his services. If the business will not provide him an adequate salary *plus* a satisfactory return on the capital he invests, he may be better off financially to work as an employee and invest his money elsewhere.

Depreciation. The buyer should pay close attention to any writeoff for depreciation expense. The amount of depreciation expense claimed is basically a decision based on the judgment of the seller and his accountant as to which method to use in computing depreciation.

Common ownership. In some cases, the buyer may find that the business is one of a group of businesses under common ownership. If this is the case, the buyer should make certain that the business has been charged for all expenses that should be attributed to it. For example, has the business been charged for its clerical and bookkeeping services, or have these been supplied by the parent company at a nominal charge or no charge at all? If they have been supplied by the parent company, the income statement should be adjusted to include this expense.

Occupancy charge. Another item about which the buyer should be concerned is the occupancy charge. Is it unusually low? This might happen for any of several reasons. Probably the most common reason is that the seller owns the property and, once it had been fully depreciated, entered no charge for rent or depreciation. If this happens, an unrealistically high net income may be reported.

Another possibility is that the business may have been paying an abnormally high or low rent for the real property occupied. This situation often occurs when the business is one of a group of businesses with common ownership.

The buyer should take care that a realistic charge for occupancy of real property is included in the adjusted income statement.

Notes to Financial Statements

A financial statement may or may not have accompanying notes. If there are notes, they should be considered an integral part of the statement and read carefully. Often important contingent liabilities or contractual obligations are described in such notes. Unless the notes are read and interpreted, the analysis of the financial statements will be incomplete.

Incorrectly Prepared Financial Statements

Many financial statements prepared by small businesses are not prepared in conformity with generally accepted accounting principles. Often no clear distinction is made, for example, between the operations of the business and the owner's personal business affairs. Such items as gasoline and car expenses that are actually personal living expenses of the owner of the business may be recorded as a business expense. The balance sheet may include as an asset the personal residence of the owner of the business. There may also be some items of business expense that were not recorded in the financial statements.

The buyer should keep in mind that the statements are only as reliable as the information that went into them. If the information is only estimated or is overstated or understated, the statements will reflect the inaccuracy. They should be adjusted to bring them as nearly as possible into line with accepted accounting principles.

Accrual Method of Accounting

If financial statements were prepared strictly on a cash basis, all cash inflow would be revenue and all cash paid out would be expense. Even fixed plant and equipment assets would be recorded as expense items at the time they were paid for instead of being charged off over the life of the assets through depreciation charges. Under the accrual method, all items of income are included in gross income *when earned,* even though payment is not received at that time. Expenses are deducted *as soon as they are incurred,* whether or not they are paid for at that time.

Normally, the accrual method of accounting is the only one that shows results of past operations accurately. If the seller's financial statements have been prepared on a cash basis, the buyer should make whatever adjustments are necessary to convert the statements to an accrual basis.

Chapter 11

Analyzing the
Financial Statements

WHEN THE FINANCIAL STATEMENTS have been made as accurate as possible, the buyer or his accountant should analyze the information they contain. Some comparisons and ratios that can be used to bring out trends and relations are discussed in this chapter.

Probably the first analysis to be made is to compare financial statements for the past 10 years or as close to that length of time as possible. Has the trend over the years been up or down, or has there been no significant change? All items on the statements should be studied.

The changes from one year to another will be more helpful if they are stated in percentages. On each year's income statement, the net sales figure is taken as 100 percent and each other item is stated as a percent of net sales. On the balance sheet, total assets are taken as 100 percent and other items are stated as percents of total assets. Such statements are called "common size" statements. Typical comparative statements covering 2 years, with common-size percents, are shown in schedules 1 and 2 (pages 86 and 87).

Ratios and Other Analyses

Certain ratios and other expressions showing relations between items on the financial statements are also helpful in interpreting the statements. Schedule 3 (page 88) illustrates several commonly used formulas based on the 1998 figures in schedules 1 and 2. Each of them is discussed briefly beginning on page 87.

Schedule 1

Comparative Balance Sheet

December 31, 1998 and December 31, 1997

	Amount		*Percent*	
	1998	*1997*	*1998*	*1997*
ASSETS				
Current assets:				
Cash......................	$14, 000	$89, 000	2. 64	18. 43
Marketable securities.........	0	80, 000	0	16. 56
Accounts receivable (net).....	68, 000	64, 000	12. 83	13. 25
Notes receivable.............	4, 000	1, 500	0. 76	0. 31
Inventories.................	190, 000	184, 000	35. 86	38. 10
Prepaid expenses............	5, 800	6, 000	1. 09	1. 24
Total current assets............	281, 800	424, 500	53. 18	87. 89
Property, plant, and equipment (net).......................	198, 100	38, 500	37. 38	7. 97
Intangibles..................	50, 000	20, 000	9. 44	4. 14
Total assets..................	$529, 900	$483, 000	100. 00	100. 00

	1998	*1997*	*1998*	*1997*
LIABILITIES AND OWNERS' EQUITY				
Current liabilities:				
Accounts payable............	$50, 400	$60, 000	9. 51	12. 42
Notes payable...............	0	10, 000	0	2. 07
Accrued taxes payable.......	800	1, 200	0. 15	0. 25
Unearned revenues..........	3, 000	0	0. 57	0
Total current liabilities........	54, 200	71, 200	10. 23	14. 74
Mortgage payable............	60, 000	10, 000	11. 32	2. 07
Total liabilities...............	114, 200	81, 200	21. 55	16. 81
Owners' equity:				
Original investment..........	250, 000	250, 000	47. 18	51. 76
Retained earnings...........	165, 700	151, 800	31. 27	31. 43
Total owners' equity...........	415, 700	401, 800	78. 45	83. 19
Total liabilities and owners' equity..............	$529, 900	$483, 000	100. 00	100. 00

Comparative Income Statement

Years ended December 31, 1997 and 1998

	Amount		Percent	
	1998	*1997*	*1998*	*1997*
Gross sales..................	$973, 500	$853, 000	101. 41	101. 21
Sales returns................	13, 500	10, 200	1. 41	1. 21
Net sales....................	960, 000	842, 800	100. 00	100. 00
Less cost of goods sold........	715, 000	622, 500	74. 48	73. 86
Gross margin...............	245, 000	220, 300	25. 52	26. 14
Operating expenses:				
Wages paid...............	141, 400	121, 500	14. 72	14. 41
Taxes....................	32, 500	31, 000	3. 38	3. 68
Insurance................	24, 000	24, 000	2. 50	2. 85
Telephone................	2, 400	2, 200	0. 25	0. 26
Miscellaneous............	5, 400	2, 750	0. 58	0. 33
Total operating expenses.....	205, 700	181, 450	21. 43	21. 53
Net income before				
taxes..............	$39, 300	$38, 850	4. 09	4. 61

Current ratio. This ratio compares current assets to current liabilities. In the example shown in schedule 3, there is $5.20 in current assets for every $1 of current liabilities.

The current ratio establishes an important relation between the business' current debt and its ability to pay the debt. The assumption is that a company should be comfortably able to pay current debts from current assets if necessary. In many businesses, however, especially service businesses, current assets are proportionately smaller because there is little inventory. In these businesses, the relation of current assets to current liabilities may be less important.

Acid test or quick ratio. This ratio points out the relation between the current assets that can be most quickly converted into cash and current liabilities. It is similar to the current ratio except that it uses only assets that are just one step away from being cash.

"One step away from cash" means that only one additional transaction is needed to convert the asset into cash. For example, accounts receivable only have to be collected and marketable securities sold.

Merchandise inventories that are normally sold on credit, on the other hand, are two steps away from cash. The inventory will first be sold and accounts receivable created. Then the accounts receivable must be collected before cash is realized from the inventory.

Days' sales uncollected. Days' sales uncollected shows how fast a business collects its accounts receivable. One way to find this figure is to divide the year-end accounts receivable by the total charge sales for the year and multiply the results by 365.

Schedule 3

Ratios and Percents

Current ratio

$$\frac{\text{Current assets, \$281,800}}{\text{Current liabilities, \$54,200}} = 5.2 \text{ to } 1.$$

Acid test or "quick ratio"

$$\frac{\text{Cash plus assets near cash, \$86,000}}{\text{Current liabilities, \$54,200}} = 1.6 \text{ to } 1.$$

Days' sales uncollected

$$\frac{\text{Accounts receivable, \$68,000}}{\text{Charge sales, \$973,500}} \times 365 = 25.5 \text{ days' sales uncollected.}$$

Turnover of merchandise inventory

$$\frac{\text{Cost of goods sold, \$715,000}}{\text{Average merchandise inventory, \$187,000}} = 3.82 \text{ times, merchandise turnover.}$$

Return on owners' investment

$$\frac{\text{Net income, \$39,300}}{\text{Beginning owners' equity, \$401,800}} = 0.0978, \text{ or } 9.78 \text{ percent, return on investment.}$$

Return on total assets invested

$$\frac{\text{Net income, \$39,300}}{\text{Total assets, \$529,900}} = 0.0742, \text{ or } 7.42 \text{ percent, return on assets invested.}$$

Owners' percentage equity in business

$$\frac{\text{Owners' equity, \$415,700}}{\text{Total assets, \$529,900}} = 0.7845, \text{ or } 78.45 \text{ percent.}$$

Creditors' percentage equity in business

$$\frac{\text{Creditors' equity, \$114,200}}{\text{Total assets, \$529,900}} = 0.2155, \text{ cr } 21.55 \text{ percent.}$$

For this computation to be valid, the accounts receivable must be fairly constant throughout the year. In most businesses, however, sales—and therefore accounts receivable also—tend to be higher at certain times of the year. It is better to use an average if possible.

Turnover of merchandise inventory. The turnover of merchandise inventory is the number of times the average inventory is sold during an accounting period. To find it, divide the cost of goods sold during the period covered by an average merchandise inventory at cost. A high turnover is usually a mark of good merchandising; but if the business only computes its inventory once a year, and that at the low point of the business's cycle, the turnover may appear better than it really is.

Return on owner's investment. The ratio of net income to proprietorship measures the owner's success in making a profit on the money he has invested in the business. Usually, net income after taxes and owner's equity as of the beginning of the year are used. (The beginning figure for any year is the December 31 figure for the year before.) If the owner's equity fluctuated greatly during the period, an average owner's equity should be used.

Return on total assets. This shows the return on the total investment of all who have a stake in the business, creditors as well as the owners.

Owner's percent of equity. For this percent, the year-end owner's equity is divided by the total assets. The share of the assets of a business contributed by the owner is always of interest to anyone trying to analyze the business. Creditors like to see a high proportion of ownership equity—the greater the owner's equity in proportion to that of the creditors, the greater the losses that can be absorbed by the owner before the creditors begin to suffer a loss.

Creditors' percent of equity. The ratio of creditor's claims to total assets is always 100 percent minus the owner's percent of equity.

Interpretation of Ratios and Percentages

The value of these ratios and percentages lies mainly in their use as tools of comparison rather than in their absolute values. Thus, a constistent increase or decrease in the current ratios of a business over a 5-year period establishes a pattern that may be significant. Suppose the current ratios for the 5 years are 7 to 1, 5 to 1, 4 to 1, 3 to 1, and 2 to 1. Clearly, the ability of the business to meet its current debt is declining.

Another important use of ratios is to compare the company's performance with that of similar businesses. For almost every size and type of business, there are published ratios of expenses to sales that are accepted throughout the industry. A comparison between the ratios of the business offered for sale and averages for the trade will bring out any discrepancies. Some of the discrepancies may be due simply to poor management, but each one should be investigated.

Evaluation of Past Years' Profits

In using a net-profit figure for past years to project the future earning potential of the business, the buyer or seller should exclude the profit of any year that is unusually high or low because of exceptional circumstances. It may also be wise to use a weighted average for the past years' profits.

Assume, for example, that two similar businesses are to be compared. Their profits for the past 5 years have been as follows:

Year	Company A	Company B
1	$9,000	$1,000
2	7,000	3,000
3	5,000	5,000
4	3,000	7,000
5	1,000	9,000
Total	$25,000	$25,000
Average	$5,000	$5,000

Both businesses show the same average profits over the 5 years and would therefore, on the basis of a simple average, be valued at the same figure. But while company A has been declining, company B has been growing. Some method is needed that will give more emphasis to the profits of the later years.

A weighted average can have this effect. How much the later profits are emphasized over the earlier years will depend on what multiplier is used, and the choice of multiplier is a matter of personal opinion. Here is an example of how a weighted average could be used to give effect to trends in comparing companies A and B:

Year	Company A			Company B		
1	$9,000 $\times$ 1 =	$ 9,000		$1,000 $\times$ 1 =	$1,000	
2	7,000 $\times$ 2 =	14,000		3,000 $\times$ 2 =	6,000	
3	5,000 $\times$ 3 =	15,000		5,000 $\times$ 3 =	15,000	
4	3,000 $\times$ 4 =	12,000		7,000 $\times$ 4 =	28,000	
5	1,000 $\times$ 5 =	5,000		9,000 $\times$ 5 =	45,000	
Total	15	$55,000		15	$95,000	
Weighted av	$55,000 $\div$ 15 = $3,667			$95,000 $\div$ 15 = $6,333		

In assessing the future of the business, the buyer must take into consideration any changes he plans to make in the basic financial structure of the business, such as putting in additional capital or not buying all the assets. However, he should not pay for future profits he is going to earn by reason of his own special skills or additional investment. In determining the future income he is purchasing, therefore, he must rely largely on past results of the business operation.

Effect of Changes in Price Levels

When the buyer is analyzing several years' financial statements, he must keep in mind the effect on the statements of changes in price levels; that is, in the purchasing power of money. He should consider the possibility of converting the amounts on the financial statements to a base year.

Putting a Value on Goodwill

Goodwill, when it exists, is a valuable asset. It may result from a good reputation, a convenient location, efficient and courteous treatment of customers, or other causes. However, because it is intangible and difficult to measure, goodwill is sometimes recorded when it does not exist.

From the accountants' standpoint, goodwill should be recorded only when it is purchased. It should not be recorded otherwise, they believe, because of the difficulty of placing a fair value on it.

As a practical matter, above-average earnings are normally considered the best evidence of the existence of goodwill, and the value placed on the goodwill at the time of its sale is often determined by capitalizing these extra earnings. Take, for example, a business in a field in which the normal return on investment is 10 percent. Suppose the business has a capital investment of $100,000 and an annual return of about $12,000. The average return on $100,000 for this type of business would be $10,000 a year. Therefore, the business has above-average earnings of $2,000 yearly.

Capitalizing these above-average earnings at 10 percent ($2,000 ÷ .10) gives $20,000 as the investment needed to earn the $2,000. Therefore $20,000 may be taken as the value of the goodwill of this firm.

Many people feel that unless a business has above-average earnings, it does not have goodwill. Thus, a business might appear to have an excellent location, enlightened customer policies, and a superb product; yet this business will not have goodwill attaching to it unless its earnings exceed the normal earnings for that type of business.

The measurement of goodwill has many pitfalls. To begin with, a decision must be made as to what normal earnings are. (Industry averages will probably be available, but *average* earnings for the industry aren't necessarily *normal* earnings.) And once this decision has been made, the percent at which the above-normal earnings will be capitalized must be decided. In the example given, 10 percent was used. This means that the buyer should recover his investment in 10 years. If he wants to recover his investment more quickly, he will want to use a higher percent, which will give a lower capitalized value. If he is willing to wait longer, he will accept a lower percent, which will raise the capitalized value.

Goodwill is simply a bookkeeping device to represent the value of one part of a business when that business is valued as a whole. In most cases, the total value of the business is decided without a detailed calculation of the goodwill figure—in many cases, without even detailed consideration of the value of the other assets.

Checklist

1. Get financial statements for the past 10 years or as long as the business has been in operation.
2. Make whatever revaluations of the financial statements are necessary to make the statements realistic.
3. Prepare ratios and percentages as needed.
4. Compare results of the company's operations from year to year in the past and with results in the industry at large.

Questions To Be Considered by the Buyer

1. What will happen to the profit when I take over the business?
2. How good is the accounting system that has been used?
3. How good is the cost system?
4. How realistic are the budgets?
5. How much owner's personal expense has been charged to or absorbed by the business?
6. Is there an equipment record—for insurance and to tell me what it costs to maintain various types of machinery?
7. Is the insurance adequate?
8. What have the financing arrangements been, particularly if sources other than a bank were used?
9. What is the rate of return on capital invested and what rate of return do I want for my capital investment?

Part 5

Analyzing the Market
Position of the Company

Introduction

Market Analysis

EVERY BUYER, and indeed every seller, should have some measurement of what the future will offer. This includes not only the possibility of maintaining the same volume of sales as in the past, but also the opportunity to increase sales.

The buyer must have some idea of what he is acquiring besides the physical assets of the business. He is, in fact, investing in or obligating himself to the continued operation of the business. The true value to him lies in the ability of the business to generate sales at least equal to its current position in the market. This calls for a careful investigation and analysis of two factors: (1) the past growth of the company within the market of which it is a part, and (2) a forecast of the future sales pattern.

The seller also needs a market analysis for the business he proposes to sell. He wants the best possible price for the business—and the better the outlook, the more likely the buyer is to agree to the asking price.

Who Does the Work?

Will a single market analysis fill the needs of both buyer and seller? Separate studies are probably better. The seller has access to data about the business that are not available to the buyer. Unless the buyer has had wide and recent experience in the same kind of business, he may—rightly or wrongly—tend to rely on the seller's statement of the market position of the company.

No two studies of the same company will produce exactly the same results. The buyer's analysis is almost certain to be on the conservative side, and a compromise will be necessary.

Another question is whether the buyer and seller should conduct their own market studies or hire specialists to do it. The detailed and complex type of investigation conducted by a professional market analyst is valuable, of course, but the cost is considerable.

The basic purpose of a market analysis in the buy-sell situation is to get a clearer picture of the company in the marketing scheme and some indication of the general direction in which it is moving. The buyer and seller should be able to gather and analyze the basic data they need for this purpose—if they avoid a highly statistical approach.

Organizing the Study

Part 5 includes five series of questions and a checklist to guide the buyer or seller in his analysis of the market position of the business. The

Sample rating charts

COMPANY SALES:

Year	Dollar sales	Percent change
1995.	$_____	_____
1996.	_____	_____
1997.	_____	_____
1998	_____	_____
1999.	_____	_____
Dollar increase 1999 over 1995. .	$_____	
Percent increase 1999 over 1995.		_____

How satisfactory?   1   2   3   4   5

SHARE OF MARKET:

Year	Industry sales	Company sales	Share of market (percent)
1995	$_____	$_____	_____
1996	_____	_____	_____
1997	_____	_____	_____
1998	_____	_____	_____
1999.	_____	_____	_____

Change in share of market 1999 over 1995 _____

How satisfactory?   1   2   3   4   5

list of questions is not complete, and not all of those given will be equally useful for all types of businesses. The nature of the business determines what kind of information is needed and in what detail. The questions will, however, call attention to some aspects of the market that might otherwise be overlooked.

Determining how important to the business a specific market characteristic is presents a problem. What is vital to one company may be unimportant to another. And some system should be worked out for rating each characteristic.

A possible method for this is to list the major subject areas in the study, showing their relative importance, and then to rate them according to a uniform system—a rating scale using numbers, for instance, or words such as "high," "medium," "low," and "not significant." An example of how a numbered scale might work in rating the company's sales over time (one of the characteristics most likely to be studied) is shown in the box on page 96.

Chapter 12

The Market

THE STRENGTH OF A MARKET depends on three elements: population, income, and motivation or attitude. The first two can be measured with some accuracy and predicted statistically. Motivation, being subjective, cannot be easily observed and is largely unpredictable.

Population in the Market Area

Population, particularly the pattern within the given market, is a dominant element in the market prospects of a business. Changes in age distribution of the population will be important to some types of businesses. Migratory factors such as shifts from rural to urban and from urban to suburban may determine the future growth of others.

Many businesses, such as food stores, will be influenced principally by the total growth in population. Others will feel the impact of structural changes—the older group with its special requirements, the increase in the infant market.

Rapidly growing communities show a larger-than-normal proportion of young families; areas with a static or declining population, a larger-than-normal proportion of older families. How permanent the population in the market is must be considered. In areas where employment is seasonal or cyclical, a large part of the population may be only semipermanent.

An analysis of population consists of more than simply counting noses. It requires a careful study of both qualitative and quantitative characteristics.

Questions in the Analysis of Population

1. *What has been the change in total population in this market area over the past 10 years?*

A comparison of census figures will show these changes. The use of census tracts in major metropolitan market areas is helpful. Many city and county government units compile population figures on various geographical bases.

2. *Using a given year in the past as a base, what has been the annual and cumulative percent of change in population in this market area?*

The cumulative percent of change is found by dividing each succeeding year by the first year. It shows as a percent how each year up to the present compares with the base year. Plotting the figures on a graph helps to visualize the progressive change.

3. *What is the average family size? Has this been increasing or decreasing?*

In many consumer-goods businesses, the size of the average family unit may be more important than total population, particularly where there are observed changes in family size. Increase in the size of the family unit has had a profound effect on many classes of consumer goods, from station wagons to outdoor gym sets.

4. *What is the population in this market measured in family units?*

The rate of change in family units will not be the same as the rate of change in total population if the size of the average family unit is changing.

5. *What is the current distribution by age groups in the market? How has this distribution changed in the past 10 years?*

Nationwide, the age distribution of the population is not the same as it was a few years ago. The under-5 and over-65 groups probably show the greatest rate of change. The buyer should know whether the seller has been alert to these changing patterns and is taking advantage of them.

6. *What percent of the population in this market can be classified as urban, suburban, rural? How has this changed over the past 10 years?*

Changing living patterns and habits change the demand patterns for various types of goods and services. If population shifts are changing the market or shows signs of being about to do so, the businessman must try to determine how much effect this has or is likely to have on his operation.

7. *What percent of the family units in this market have only one person? Two? Three? Four? More?*

A breakdown of family units by number of persons in the family has value for businesses whose sales volume is at least somewhat related to family size. A manufacturer of outdoor portable swimming pools, for instance, would be interested in family sizes because this would influence the production of various sizes of pools.

8. *What percent of the total population or family units are potential customers for this kind of business?*

This is particularly important for businesses whose goods or services are related to the way people live. The demand for three-horsepower garden tractors will depend on the number of families living on small acreages. Septic tank sales will depend on the families not eligible for public sewerage services. An analysis of the market for specialized goods and services may be the key to evaluating the future of the business.

9. *How has the total population been changing over the past 10 years? Is it—*

> *Increasing at an increasing rate?*
> *Increasing at a decreasing rate?*
> *Showing no change?*
> *Decreasing at a decreasing rate?*
> *Decreasing at an increasing rate?*

Population may be continuing to increase, but at a slower rate. This would probably suggest less *in*-migration and more *out*-migration, or perhaps a reduced birth rate, though this would probably occur over a fairly long period of time. Analysis of vital statistics of the market (births over deaths) is advisable.

10. *What is the level of education in the market? Is it increasing? What is the rate of increase? What is the level of education by age groups in the adult population? Education of the male population? Female population?*

Generally, the higher the education level, the higher the income level is likely to be, with correspondingly greater capacity for goods and services. Trends in the level of education, particularly when correlated with income, may indicate future potential.

Income in the Market Area

Income as used here refers to net spendable income rather than gross earnings. Of the spendable income, the primary concern is with that which remains after fixed or relatively fixed obligations have been met—rent or home payments, utility payments, insurance premiums, and the like. The amount left is the income over which the consumer has some control—whether to spend all of it or some.

How each consumer spends this income is largely a matter of personal motivation. The total amount available for consumption in the market, however, depends on the economic factors influencing income. Variations in total income and the resulting purchasing power stem largely from two sources: (1) changes in the average income of the family unit, with the same general level of employment prevailing; and (2) changes in the level of employment with the average income constant.

The difference between earned income and real income must also be recognized. If the cost of living is increasing at a rate about equal to the purchasing power, there is no gain in purchasing power. Dollar purchases may increase, but each dollar buys less. The net difference between the increase in income and the increase in prices reflects the true gain or loss in income converted to purchasing power.

Some classes of goods and services show no positive relation between demand and income levels. For example, when incomes rise, more dollars are spent for food, but the *percent* of income channeled into these goods is smaller.

Income is important in market analysis because changes in income are reflected in the demand patterns for goods and services. No business is free from this effect. As barbershop prices increase, the interval between haircuts increases and the sale of hair clippers for home use rises. The demand for funerals in a rising market does not change, but the degree of ornateness in the casket or services decreases.

Questions in the Analysis of Income

1. *What is the total spendable income within the market area? What is the average per capita income? Average per family income?*

2. *What has been the rate of change in income (per capita, per family) over the past 10 years on both a year-to-year basis and a cumulative basis?*

Changes in income reflect the changing status of the market. The change is most likely to be an increase, but the extent of the increase should be known.

3. *How does the rate of change in income in this market compare with changes in the Nation as a whole and in similar markets?*

The economic factors affecting the income status of a given market may differ from those at work in the economy as a whole, but it is helpful to know how changes in this market compare with trends in other markets.

4. What is the distribution of income and purchasing power by income class in the market?

A frequency distribution such as this can be used to analyze income and purchasing power:

Distribution	Percent of family units	Percent of total purchasing power
$0 to $2,499	_____	_____
$2,500 to $3,999	_____	_____
$4,000 to $6,999	_____	_____
$7,000 to $9,999	_____	_____
$10,000 and over	_____	_____

The $4,000 to $6,999 income group, for instance, might represent 32 percent of all family units and 38 percent of the purchasing power; the $10,000-and-over group, 5 percent of the family units and 11 percent of the purchasing power. The higher-income groups will ordinarily be smaller, but they will have a higher-than-proportionate purchasing power.

5. How has the distribution of income and purchasing power by income classes changed over the past 10 years?

This information should be reduced to year-to-year and cumulative percentages.

6. What are the types of employment and the percentage of the working force in each class?

Here, again, changes over time should be studied.

7. Have there been any significant changes in the forms of employment in this market over the past 10 years? What changes in industry and employment in this market are foreseeable?

8. What is the level of unemployment in this market area? Is unemployment increasing? Decreasing? Showing no appreciable change?

Knowledge of the unemployment trend is important because of the direct effect it has on purchasing power and the psychological effect of the threat of unemployment.

9. How much do consumers typically spend for various classes of goods and services in this kind of market?

Competition in the Market Area

The buyer of a business not only acquires the physical property of the company; he also inherits its competition. He will probably be able to do little or nothing to lessen the competitive pressure operating against him, but he can develop a clear working knowledge of what he will face—the state of competition, the relative strength of the business within the market, the general patterns of development and change. A detailed analysis of the competition is highly desirable in deciding whether to buy an existing business.

Attention should be given first to competitors of about the same type and size as the business in question, since they are on a more realistic level of competition. A small clothing store would be wise to concern itself with other small clothing stores rather than with a high-volume department store. In time, a small operation might grow to the point of competing successfully with major firms, but the immediate pull of competition will come from other businesses of about the same size and description.

Investigation of large businesses, if any is made, should concern the extent to which they enlarge the total market, stimulate demand, or otherwise open up market possibilities to the smaller business.

Questions in the Analysis of Competition

1. *How many competitive businesses are there within the market area of this business? Where are they located? What can be found out about them? From whom?*

The market area in this sense is the trade area in which the business operates. In a retail, wholesale, or service business, this trade area may be rather narrowly defined. In a manufacturing or mail-order business, there may be a number of markets—regional, national, and perhaps even international.

Markets can be further defined as either consumer-goods markets or industrial-goods markets, depending on the nature of the business and the goods or services with which it deals. The market or markets must be carefully identified to avoid any waste of time and effort in making the analysis.

2. *How many competitive businesses have gone out of business or moved out of the market area within the past year?*

If there has been a decline in the number of competitors, an attempt should be made to find out why. If the decline has been significant, it may indicate that there are too many businesses of that type for the potential sales volume. If other areas of the analysis tend to indicate a declining market, exodus of competing businesses may help support those findings.

3. *How many competitive businesses have opened in this market area within the past year?*

Is this increase in competition more than should normally be expected? What circumstances have been responsible for the increase in competition? Can the market support all these businesses?

Unless the market grows in proportion to new competitive entries, the net result is a smaller share for each competitor.

4. What is the total known or estimated volume of competitive business within the market area?

This should give a cross-check on the volume of business done by the company up for sale. The total sales estimate for the market less that done by the company gives a reasonably accurate estimate of the volume going to the competition. Or the sales of the company can be estimated by subtracting competitors' sales from total sales in the market.

5. What sort of sales effort does the competition make?

How do the competitors advertise, promote? What advertising media are used? How much?

What is the quality of competitors' sales forces? Could business be drawn from competitors by improving on their sales ability?

There is likely to be considerable variation in the level of sales effort between competitors in the same market, from those who are highly aggressive to those who simply "follow the crowd." The person investigating the market should analyze competition from this point of view as intensively as possible.

6. What is the total footage of all competitive businesses within the market area?

From the total gross footage and total estimated volume, it is possible to get an overall sales-per-square-foot average to compare with the company under consideration.

7. What is the general physical appearance of competitive establishments in the market area?

Generally speaking, alert, progressive firms present an up-to-date physical appearance and use the newest techniques of operation. A generally high level of overall appearance gives some indication of the aggressiveness of the competition.

8. What other competitive businesses are known to be for sale within the market area?

If general business conditions are such that other competitors are seeking to get out of the market, the prospective buyer should know it. It may signify that the area is not a good one for entering business. On the other hand, a lessening of competition leaves to the business in question a larger potential volume. The reasons why competitors have left the market area should be learned. A decision to purchase assumes economic health in the market.

9. *What other kinds of businesses are in indirect competition—that is, deal at least to some extent in the same kinds of goods or services as the business being considered for sale or purchase?*

Businesses are constantly adding lines of merchandise, expanding services offered, and creating new products. As a result, the pattern of competition changes rapidly. The buyer, and presumably the seller, should be aware of these changes and their likely effect on the business in question.

10. *Can the competitive businesses be rated, taking all factors into account, from the strongest or most dominant to the weakest?*

What characteristics of the strongest competitors should be studied with an eye to improving the business being bought or sold? What weaknesses of the competition might the buyer or seller be able to capitalize on?

11. *What kinds of services to customers are competitors offering that this business does not?*

Customer services are becoming a dominant force in attracting and holding customers. Services offered to customers by competitors should be investigated carefully to determine the effect these have on attracting sales volume.

12. *What are the general pricing policies of competitors?*

An actual price comparison of specific products or services should be made. Attention should be concentrated on general price levels rather than specific items—the purpose is to compare this company and its competition, taking into account cost of merchandise, relation with sources of supply, cost of operation and so on.

13. *How influential has the competition been in enlarging the overall market?*

Demand is classified in two ways: primary demand, which is the demand for certain *kinds* of goods or services, and selective demand, which is demand for a given *brand* or desire to purchase from a *specific company*. Competition, through promotion and sales effort, must be able to enlarge market capacity for a product by type or class. The combined sales effort of all appliance stores in a market, for example, will expand the primary demand for air conditioning. Thus the separate but total force of competition may have the positive effect of expanding the basic market.

105

14. *How does the competition compare with the business in the buy-sell transaction as to the amount apparently spent on sales effort?*

The nature and extent of advertising and promotion is often a strong indicator of the competitive intensity of business within a market. As the market becomes more competitive, sales-effort costs as a percentage of sales tend to rise. A study of competitive advertising and promotion—the media and methods used, the form the promotion follows—would be of value in the market analysis.

15. *Is there evidence of concerted or cooperative effort on the part of the competition to increase the total market?*

Through trade associations? Joint promotional programs? How effective does the effort appear to be?

Chapter 13

The Company

J UST AS IMPORTANT as a study of the market as a whole is a study of the position in that market of the company under consideration and how well it has performed under existing conditions.

Location

When a brand new business is being opened, the prospective owner has some choice about location. In buying a going concern, this is seldom possible. The seller is not likely to sell the assets of the firm with the understanding that the buyer will find other premises. Neither is it likely that the buyer will acquire the assets and then seek other quarters from which to operate. Location, then, remains as it is at the time of the buy-sell transaction. The buyer should give careful thought to the location of the business he is considering, particularly in relation to the market of which it is a part.

Questions in the Analysis of Location

1. *Is there any possibility that the status of this location will change in the foreseeable future?*

Urban renewal programs, for example, have a direct effect on business locations as well as on residential buildings. The buyer should look carefully into the possibility that the area will become a target for urban development that would require him to vacate the premises. The same investigation should be made in connection with other forms of development that might cause land condemnation or change of status—highways, flood-control projects, military uses, rezoning, and the like.

2. What specific factors should be examined in determining the desirability of the location?

The following outline suggests points that should be considered in evaluating the location of a retail store. It can be adapted for use with other types of businesses.

Checklist for Locating a Store

City or Town

1. Economic considerations

   Industry
   > Farming
   > Manufacturing
   > Trading

   Trend
   > Highly satisfactory
   > Growing
   > Stationary
   > Declining

   Permanency
   > Old and well established
   > Old and reviving
   > New and promising
   > Recent and uncertain

   Diversification
   > Many and varied industries
   > Many of the same type
   > Few but varied
   > Dependent on one industry

   Stability
   > Constant
   > Satisfactory
   > Average
   > Subject to wide fluctuations

   Seasonality
   > Little or no seasonal change
   > Mild seasonal change
   > Periodic—every few years
   > Highly seasonal in nature

Future
  Very promising
  Satisfactory
  Uncertain
  Poor outlook

2. Population

  Income distribution
    Mostly wealthy
    Well distributed
    Mostly middle income
    Poor

  Trend
    Growing
    Large and stable
    Small and stable
    Declining

  Living status
    Own homes
    Pay substantial rent
    Pay moderate rent
    Pay low rent

3. Competition

  Number of competing stores
    Few
    Average
    Many
    Too many

  Type of management
    Not progressive
    Average
    Above average
    Alert and progressive

  Presence of chains
    No chains
    Few chains
    Average number
    Many well established

  Type of competing stores
    Unattractive
    Average
    Old and well established
    Are many people shopping outside the community?

4. The town as a place to live

Character of the city
Are homes neat and clean, or run down and shabby?
Are lawns, parks, streets, and so on neat, modern, and generally attractive?
Are adequate facilities available?
Banking
Transportation
Professional services
Utilities
Schools
Churches
Amusement centers
Medical and dental services
Is the climate satisfactory for the type of business you are considering?

The Site

1. Competition

Number of independent stores of the same kind as yours
Same block
Same side of the street
Across the street

Number of chain stores
In the same block
Same side of the street
Across the street

Kind of stores next door

Number of vacancies
Same side of the street
Across the street
Next door

Dollar sales of your nearest competitor

2. Traffic flow

Sex of pedestrians
Age of pedestrians
Destination of pedestrians
Number of passersby
Automobile traffic count
Peak hours of traffic flow

3. Transportation

  Transfer points
  Highway
  Kind (bus, streetcar, auto, railroad)

4. Parking facilities

  Large and convenient
  Large enough but not convenient
  Convenient but too small
  Completely inadequate

5. Side of street

6. Plant

  Frontage and depth—in feet
  Shape of building
  Condition
  Heat—type, air conditioning
  Light
  Display space
  Front and back entrances
  Display windows

7. Corner location—if not, what is it?

8. Unfavorable characteristics

  Fire hazards
  Cemetery
  Hospital
  Industry
  Relief office
  Undertaker
  Vacant lot—without parking possibilities
  Garages
  Playground
  Smoke, dust, odors
  Poor sidewalks and pavement
  Unsightly neighborhood buildings

9. Professional men in block

  Medical doctors and dentists
  Lawyers
  Veterinarians
  Others

10. History of the site

Sales Effort

The discussion here concerns the nature of the company's sales effort and measurement of its cost against the resulting sales. For practical purposes, selling effort can be classified as indirect and direct. *Indirect* sales effort includes all forms of nonpersonal customer-oriented advertising and promotion. *Direct* sales effort is the performance of persons directly engaged in selling the merchandise or services offered.

Questions in the Analysis of Sales Effort

1. *How much was spent for advertising during the past year? How much per year for the past 10 years?*

These figures should be reduced to percent of change so that the results over time can be studied.

2. *What advertising media were used and what percent or estimated percent of the total advertising expenditures went to each medium?*

> *Newspapers?*
> *Trade papers?*
> *Magazines—kinds of magazines?*
> *Broadcast media—radio, television?*
> *Other forms of advertising?*

The question is whether the media being used are a reasonable choice considering the amount that can be spent.

3. *What changes have been made in the use of advertising media? Is the company relying more on one form of advertising than in the past? If so, why the change?*

No one advertising medium is best for all types of businesses. There is sometimes a tendency, however, to switch media too often, without giving any medium enough time to show its real value.

4. *How does the cycle of advertising vary in relation to seasonal sales fluctuations? As sales increase, do advertising costs increase in about the same proportion? What is the pattern?*

Dollar advertising expenditures usually rise as sales volume rises but not as fast percentagewise. When sales drop, there is a tendency to spend either too much or too little in relation to normal seasonal changes, depending on the urgency felt by the advertiser.

5. *If advertising allowances are available from vendors or sources of supply, is the company taking advantage of them? What kinds are available?*

Advertising allowances, if properly used, make it possible to do more advertising with less money. An alert advertiser will take advantage of all advertising allowances he feels to be reasonable and useful to his business.

6. *Is the company taking advantage of other available promotional services such as newspaper mats and so on?*

Many suppliers offer advertising services that help improve the quality of the advertising, reduce the cost, or perhaps both. The company's use of all advertising and promotional helps should be analyzed.

7. *What percent of sales was spent on advertising last year? For the past 10 years? Is this increasing? Decreasing?*

It is important to know not only changes in the pattern of advertising expenditures, but the relation between these changes and changes in sales volume.

8. *How do the advertising and promotion costs of this business compare with typical or average figures for this kind of business? Higher? Lower? About the same?*

Figures are available from trade sources and other reporting agencies that will give a standard of comparison.

9. *Are other forms of promotion being used effectively? Window display? Interior layout and display?*

For many kinds of businesses, other promotion methods may be as important as media advertising, or even more so. All possibilities should be studied as to their importance in the business under consideration.

10. *Is the company capitalizing on all special promotion events suitable to the business?*

This point covers a wide range of activity. Examples might be maximizing sales effort at the seasonal peak or peaks of the business, using trading stamps or other premiums, participating with sources of supply in special promotions, and so on.

11. *What percent of sales has gone into selling-payroll costs for the past 10 years? What has been the trend? Are selling costs increasing, decreasing, remaining about the same?*

Changes in selling costs should be studied singly, in comparison to changes in sales volume, and in comparison to standards or averages for businesses of the same kind.

12. *What is the quality of the selling effort of this company as shown by such factors as training, sales attitude, methods of compensation, and the like?*

Selling-payroll costs as a measure of sales effort do not reveal the forces at work behind this effort and affecting its quality. Motivation of sales personnel through training, method and amount of compensation, and sales management should also be considered.

Past Sales

The history of sales growth within the company and in relation to similar businesses is considered the principal measure of company progress. The buyer or seller should note three types of variations that influence sales and how each may affect the buy-sell transaction.

Seasonal fluctuations. All businesses are affected to some extent by seasonal variations in the demand for goods or services. These variations may be the result of numerous factors—buyer motivation, weather, specific events. Their nature, causes, and extent should be identified as fully as possible. Some are reasonably predictable; others are not.

The prospective buyer of a business should think in terms of completing the purchase just before the maximum seasonal peak of the company. This will give him the greatest possible short-term gain and return on investment. Buying a business immediately after the maximum seasonal peak puts an additional burden on short-term working capital.

The seller is likely to take the opposite view. He is most likely to want to sell immediately *after* the seasonal peak of the company, thus realizing the best possible profit. (It is assumed here that time in relation to sales peaks and valleys would have no appreciable effect on the market or replacement value of assets other than merchandise.)

Cyclical fluctuations. Cyclical fluctuations are changes that occur over a longer period of time but tend to appear somewhat regularly. Periods of depression and prosperity will obviously affect the future of a business. The major difficulty is to determine what effect such fluctuations will have on the businesses being bought or sold.

Long-range trends. Long-range patterns of change in an industry or a given business fall within this classification. The interplay of forces creating such trends is extremely complex, but the buyer in particular should be alert for changing patterns in his industry or market that are likely to affect the future of the business.

Questions in the Analysis of Sales

1. *What has been the year-to-year change in dollar sales?*

The length of time to use is largely a matter of judgment. If the figures are later to be used to make projections, a 10-year period or more is not unreasonable if the company has been in business that long. Converting the dollar figures to yearly percent of change and plotting them on a graph makes them easier to interpret.

2. *Using a given year in the past as a base, what has been the cumulative rate of change up to the present?*

Again, plotting the figures on a graph helps to visualize the changes.

3. *What has been the percent of change in sales, year-to-year and cumulative, for this kind of business on a national or other basis?*

The years should be comparable to those used in questions 1 and 2 so that the pattern of change for the company can be compared with that for like businesses.

4. *How much of the increase or decrease in sales can be attributed to increasing or decreasing prices and how much to real sales?*

The fact that sales have shown an increase may lead to a false conclusion that the company has shown good growth. In some types of businesses, merchandise costs have increased rapidly. An average increase of 2 percent per year in sales over 5 years changes in significance when it is known that prices have increased 8 percent during the same period. Consumer and wholesale price indexes should be checked, as well as other factors that may indicate rising prices.

5. *Have prices in this company increased more rapidly, less rapidly, or at about the same rate as those in this kind of business generally?*

It is important to know how the business compares in this respect with similar firms. If it is out of line, what is the reason?

6. *Over a period of years, what has been the change in the level of sales for this business as compared to all businesses of this type? Are sales—*

Increasing percentagewise more than normal?
Increasing at about the same rate?
Increasing less than normal?
Showing no increase at all?
Decreasing less than normal if like businesses are decreasing?
Decreasing at about the same rate?
Decreasing more than normal?

7. *What is causing the increase or decrease in sales (a) for this company and (b) for similar businesses?*

This point may prove to be the one that basically determines the decision to buy or sell the business.

8. *Has the rate of change in sales been increasing?*

Are sales increasing more rapidly now than, say, a year or two ago? Are sales increasing less rapidly now? If sales are decreasing, has the rate of decrease increased or lessened?

9. *At the time of the study, where does the business stand seasonally?*

Is this normally the low point for sales in this kind of business? Is it the high point? Somewhere in between? Is seasonal variation so minor as to have little or no significance? Are seasonal variations predictable?

Seasonal variations may have a strong bearing on when the buyer is willing to purchase, when the seller is willing to sell, and the price.

10. *What percentage of the year's business is done each month? What is the monthly average over the past several years?*

Monthly sales averages help to determine immediate working capital requirements and to plan sales for the months ahead. They are especially important when the sales of a given month as a percent of the year's total do not vary greatly from year to year. If there has been considerable variation, the reasons for it should be indentified if possible.

11. *Do there appear to be any changes in the seasonal pattern of sales? If so, what appears to be causing these changes?*

Changes in consumer buying habits, the pressure of increased competition, governmental regulations, and the like create changes over time that may affect the short-term sales cycle of the business.

12. *If a change in the seasonal pattern is occurring, does it tend to increase total sales or merely shift the volume from one month to another?*

A comparison of several years' sales may show that the overall effect is not a proportionate gain in total business but a readjustment of sales from month to month throughout the year.

13. *If cyclical changes have any effect on this kind of business, what is the nature of the fluctuations? How often do they occur? With what intensity?*

14. *Have sales of this business in the past tended to show the effect of these cyclical fluctuations? To what extent? Intensity?*

Knowing the effect of cyclical changes on the business may give some idea of what can be expected from the standpoint of intermediate-range planning and forecasting.

15. *If the business is influenced by cyclical fluctuations, at what stage is the cycle at the time of the study?*

Cyclical fluctuations may be the result of broad-scale economic circumstances, but the intermediate effect on a given business may not be in proportion to normal economic indicators.

16. *What is the ratio of operating expenses to sales in the most recent operating statement?*

A comparison of these costs with ratios or averages of similar businesses should give an indication of the operating efficiency.

17. *What has been the year-to-year and average ratio of operating expenses to sales for past years?*

Have operating expenses tended to increase, decrease, or remain about the same in relation to sales?

Has the relative change in operating expenses been about equal to, greater than, or less than the relative change in sales?

On a cumulative basis, what has been the change in the pattern of operating expenses over the past years?

18. *Are selling costs (sales, salaries, advertising, delivery) increasing, decreasing, or remaining the same in relation to sales?*

If selling costs are increasing faster than sales, each dollar spent on selling effort is bringing in a smaller return. This information may suggest possible ways of increasing the efficiency of the company's sales effort.

19. *What is the ratio of net sales to gross sales and what has been the trend of this ratio over the past years?*

An increase in the difference between net and gross sales may indicate weaknesses within the company in policy, sales effectiveness, merchandising, quality control, or a combination of two or more of these factors.

20. *What are the reasons for customer returns and allowances and what action is being taken to reduce them, if reduction is possible?*

Care should be taken in analyzing the sales of a company to see that gross sales are not taken as net sales, particularly if lenient returns and allowances have been a part of the sales program.

21. *What has been the pattern in the value of the average transaction over the past years?*

Sales may be stationary, but the number of transactions may increase or decrease, thus changing the value of the average sale. Or sales may be changing but disproportionately to transactions. The ideal to be sought is an increase both in the value of the transactions and in their number.

22. *How do transactions in this business compare in average value and number with those of similar businesses throughout the industry or market area?*

This will give a standard of comparison to show how well the company has been able to realize an average sale in terms of what it would be normal to expect.

23. *What are the current sales per square foot of floor space for the business? What has been the trend in sales per square foot for the past several years? How does this compare to known averages or ratios for other businesses of this type?*

The purpose of this analysis is to estimate how efficiently space is being used for sales purposes. It may be figured on the basis of total gross footage, including area used for other than selling purposes, or it may be limited to the space devoted primarily to selling and merchandising.

Chapter 14

The Sales Forecast

W HEN THE BUSINESS AND THE MARKET have been analyzed, the probable sales volume of the business can be forecast. This forecast should be a simple projection of the business involved; it should not be an attempt to forecast or project the total state of the market. The variables that influence the market are too vast and complex for a small businessman to do anything about. It will have to be assumed that what has happened to establish the condition of the market as it is, will continue to have the same general effect, at least for the period just ahead.

This is a dangerous assumption—markets and the economy are dynamic, not static—but from the practical point of view, there is little choice. In any case, it is usually over longer periods of time that changing market factors make themselves felt.

Sales Forecast vs. Sales Potential

A distinction is necessary here between making a sales forecast and estimating sales potential. A sales forecast is based on past sales performance and a reckoning of known and anticipated market conditions. From these, the expected sales level is determined.

Sales potential, on the other hand, is a measure of the capacity of the business to reach a certain volume of sales. It is based on knowledge of the total market and the extent of competitive influence, and it involves the use of strategy through sales effort. Past sales performance may bear little or no resemblance to sales potential. In general, sales potential is likely to represent a higher sales level than a sales forecast.

Length of the Forecast

For the purposes of a buy-sell transaction, a short-term or at most an intermediate-term forecast is all that should be attempted. Short-term forecasts cover a few months—seldom more than a year. Intermediate-term forecasts should be limited to 1 or 2 years.

The Information Needed

Since the forecast is based on past sales of the company, it is necessary to know the dollar sales volume of the firm for the past several years. If not enough sales data have been recorded, it may be necessary to improvise.

In one instance, the prospective buyer of a self-service laundry was unable to get sales figures. He contacted the manufacturer of the washing machines to determine the amount of water used per machine load. He then learned from the water company the amount of water consumed by the business. Using these two figures and making allowances for water used for drinking, rest room, and so on, he computed the number of loads washed per month. This figure multiplied by the price charged per load gave him a reasonably accurate figure for the sales volume.

Short-Term Sales Forecasting

For a short-term forecast, it is usually enough to know the sales for the past few weeks or months in comparison with the corresponding period of the year before. If sales for the past 4 weeks were 8 percent more than the corresponding 4 weeks of the preceding year, sales for the next few weeks can reasonably be expected to be 8 percent ahead of the corresponding period a year ago.

Adjustments have to be made, of course, for any known or predicted conditions that will change this rate of increase—conditions such as unusual weather, short-lived labor disputes, changes in the dates of events such as Easter, and so on.

Distribution of sales by months. A longer method of forecasting is based on the distribution of sales by months. This method works best if the monthly variations over a period of years have been small.

Suppose, for instance, that a short-term forecast is being made in June. For the past several years, sales in July have been between 11 and 13 percent of annual sales, with an average of 12.5 percent. During the same period, May sales have averaged 10 percent of annual sales. Sales during the May just past were $8,000. Then $8,000÷.10= $80,000, the estimated annual sales. Projected sales for July will be

12.5 percent of $80,000, or $10,000. Sales for other months can be forecast in the same way.

Cumulative percents. Another method of short-term forecasting is the cumulative-percent method. The percent of total sales is figured for each week during the past year and added to the percent for preceding weeks, as shown in this example:

Weeks	Weekly percent	Cumulative percent
1	.9	.9
2	1.1	2.0
3	1.4	3.4
4	1.7	5.1
5	1.9	7.0
6	2.4	9.4
7	2.6	12.0
8	2.9	14.9
9	3.1	18.0

If sales during the first 4 weeks amount to $4,000, the annual total will be estimated at $4,000÷.051, or $78,430. To forecast sales for the next 4 weeks, add the percentages for those weeks and multiply the annual estimate by the result ($78,430×.098=$7,686). This method works best for goods or services that are not subject to wide variations in sales volume and whose prices do not fluctuate greatly.

Number of sales transactions. Where prices tend to vary, the number of sales transactions may ˙how a steadier trend than dollar sales do. An increase in dollar sales without an increase in the number of transactions means that the average dollar value per transaction has gone up. This increase in the amount of the average sale may mean (1) that customers are buying higher-quality goods, (2) that they are buying in larger quantities, or (3) that prices have increased.

If the level of transactions is steadier than the dollar sales, the forecast tends to be more conservative. A study of the transactions may bring to light factors not revealed by total dollar sales.

Intermediate-Term Sales Forecasting

Because of the combination of variables at work in the market, the techniques used in the short-term forecast are not reliable when applied to the longer periods covered by intermediate-term forecasting. In the longer forecast, two methods of measurement are generally used: the long-term trend method and the correlation method. Correlation analysis requires data usually beyond the reach of the small businessman, but the long-term trend as determined by the least squares method may be useful. This method will not be taken up here, but an explanation of its use can be found in any introductory book on statistical methods.

Effect of Changing Market Factors

It must be reemphasized that a trend is determined from past data and from the total market as reflected in company sales. Insofar as these conditions remain in about the same state of balance, a projection of the trend into the future has some value; but the more dynamic these market factors are, the less reliable trend lines become.

The investigator must give careful thought to how changing market factors will affect his forecast. Although he cannot have precise knowledge of these factors, he must decide how influential they are likely to be and adjust his forecast accordingly.

A midwestern city offers an interesting example of the weaknesses of long-term trends in measuring the future. Within ten years, the population in this city increased from 165,000 to 245,500 because of a high level of employment in the aircraft industry. Then, during and following the next year, employment in aircraft production was reduced substantially. Many residents left to seek employment elsewhere, and population growth slowed down significantly. Total purchasing power reflected the economic change, and the total volume of sales increased at a substantially slower rate.

The suddenness with which this occurred, the fact that it was non-cyclical, and the general unpreparedness for it raised havoc with earlier forecasts.

Conclusions on Forecasting

The reliability of a forecast is always uncertain. Past performance is no guarantee of the future. The basic value in making a forecast is that it forces the buyer or seller to look at the future objectively. A forecast does not eliminate the need for value judgments, but it does require the forecaster to identify elements influencing the future. It may act as a damper on the buyer's unbounded faith in his own managerial ability.

"The ESSENTIALS" of
ACCOUNTING & BUSINESS

Each book in the **Accounting and Business ESSENTIALS** series offers all essential information about the subject it covers. It includes every important principle and concept, and is designed to help students in preparing for exams and doing homework. The **Accounting and Business ESSENTIALS** are excellent supplements to any class text or course of study.

The **Accounting and Business ESSENTIALS** are complete and concise, giving the reader ready access to the most critical information in the field. They also make for handy references at all times. The **Accounting and Business ESSENTIALS** are prepared with REA's customary concern for high professional quality and student needs.

Available titles include:

Accounting I & II

Advanced Accounting I & II

Advertising

Auditing

Business Law I & II

Business Statistics I & II

College & University Writing

Corporate Taxation

Cost & Managerial Accounting I & II

Financial Management

Income Taxation

Intermediate Accounting I & II

Macroeconomics I & II

Marketing Principles

Microeconomics

Money & Banking I & II

If you would like more information about any of these books,
complete the coupon below and return it to us, or visit your local bookstore.

RESEARCH & EDUCATION ASSOCIATION
61 Ethel Road W. • Piscataway, New Jersey 08854
Phone: (732) 819-8880   **website: www.rea.com**

Please send me more information about your Accounting & Business Essentials books

Name _____

Address _____

City _____ State _____ Zip _____